THE WHICH?
PROBLEMSOLVER

D0270815

THE WHICH? PROBLEMSOLVER

CASSANDRA KENT

Published by Consumers' Association
and Hodder & Stoughton

Which? Books are commissioned and researched by
The Association for Consumer Research
and published by Consumers' Association,
2 Marylebone Road, London NW1 4DF and
Hodder & Stoughton, 47 Bedford Square, London WC1B 3DP

First edition January 1993
Copyright © 1993 Consumers' Association Ltd

British Library Cataloguing in Publication Data
Kent, Cassandra
  Which? ProblemSolver
  I. Title
  640

ISBN 0 340 58115 8

Thanks for choosing this book . . .

If you find it useful, we'd like to hear from you. Even if it doesn't do
the job you were expecting, we'd still like to know. Then we can take
your comments into account when preparing similar titles or, indeed,
the next edition of the book. Address your letter to the Publishing
Manager at Consumers' Association, FREEPOST, 2 Marylebone
Road, London NW1 4DF. We look forward to hearing from you.

No part of this publication may be reproduced or transmitted in any form or
by any means, electronically or mechanically, including photocopying,
recording or any other information storage or retrieval system, without
prior permission in writing from the publisher. This publication is not
included under licences issued by the Copyright Agency.

Cover illustrations by Honeysett/Chubb Fire Ltd/Geoffrey Goode
Text illustrations by Stuart McLean
Typographic design by Paul Saunders
Typeset by Litho Link Limited, Welshpool, Powys, Wales
Printed in England by Clays Ltd, St Ives plc

Grateful thanks are also extended to RoSPA and The British Red Cross Society

CONTENTS

About the author

Cassandra Kent is a freelance journalist, author and broadcaster specialising in consumer affairs and home management.

She worked for *Which?* magazine, a broadcasting trade union and the Family Planning Association before joining *Good Housekeeping*, where she worked for some years, including a period as Director of Research and Testing of the Good Housekeeping Institute. She now writes for magazines and newspapers and is author of over twenty practical household books.

Introduction

Have you ever spilt tea, wine or ice-cream on the carpet and not known the best way to remove the stain? had to extinguish a chip-pan fire? or wondered how to eliminate the army of ants marching around your kitchen? Perhaps you have a neighbour who plays the drums at two in the morning or a tradesman has let you down by not finishing a job? Even if you're only being bothered by an endlessly dripping tap, this new guide could help you sort out the trouble quickly and effectively.

The Which? ProblemSolver is an essential reference book for busy people who want straightforward answers to everyday domestic problems. It tackles prevention as well as cure, with advice on reducing heating costs, preventing burglary and protecting the fabric of your home.

The Which? ProblemSolver offers hundreds of household tips, both traditional and modern: it describes many uses for white vinegar and soapflakes, as well as technological lifesavers, such as cleaning solvents and proprietary carpet spotting kits. It also makes sense of those mysterious laundry code symbols, to help you avoid the costly misadventure of washing a white silk shirt along with a pair of brand-new jeans.

It even tells you how to cut down on cleaning: for instance, pearls are at their best when in contact with human skin – it's the oils that help preserve their lustre; most furniture needs polishing only two or three times a year and bakeware tends to perform better the less it is washed.

The 'ingredients' you may need to keep your home in tip-top condition range from chemical products to everyday items such as orange peel, talcum powder and onions. Aluminium foil can be used for insulating the home as well as for wrapping the Christmas turkey. But, used incorrectly, even common substances can cause damage – salt used in a solution keeps bamboo furniture stiff, but if applied to carpet stains it attracts dirt to the spot.

The book also contains some first-aid essentials for the sorts of accidents that can happen, all too easily, in and around the house.

Major crises such as choking and electric shocks are covered in addition to painful but less serious predicaments such as splinters and midge bites.

Other sections are devoted to house-moving and holiday preparations, cycles and cars, and electrical and plumbing problems.

Should the worst come to the worst, the guide explains when you should call in an expert for professional help, and advises on insurance cover. It also tells you how to make a claim and explains why a claim might be refused or reduced by the insurance company.

From bleeding noses to bleeding radiators, from frozen car locks to frozen chickens and from flour beetles to flower stains, this is truly a book of which it can be said, 'Every home should have one'.

1

DOMESTIC PROBLEMS

Food and the kitchen
Marks and spills
Household and cleaning problems
Getting rid of smells
Problems with pests
Sewing and mending tips

Food and the kitchen

- Food poisoning • Hygiene
- Kitchen safety • Freezer emergencies
- Culinary crises • Microwave cooking

Forget, for a moment, about the kitchen as the heart of the home and think of it instead as the most hazardous room. In it you can have innumerable accidents – burns, scalds, cuts – and it's also the source of food poisoning.

FOOD POISONING

Food poisoning can cause severe illness and even death. Symptoms include double vision, problems with swallowing, stomach cramps, fever, vomiting, diarrhoea and a general feeling of weakness. It can occur between 2 and 36 hours of eating infected food.

Avoidance
- Keep perishable foods in the refrigerator.
- Don't refreeze defrosted food.
- Keep refrigerator and kitchen utensils scrupulously clean.
- Throw out any food that has passed its use-by-date, cans that are dented or rusty and anything that looks or smells 'off'.
- Cover food so flies can't get near it.
- Don't eat restaurant food that you suspect has been prepared unhygienically or that has been sitting around for some time at room temperature.

- Wash your hands before handling or eating food.
- Reheat food thoroughly to 70°C for a minimum of two minutes.

Recovery

- Make the sufferer as comfortable as possible.
- Give small sips of water at frequent intervals.
- When recovery starts, give bland non-greasy foods.
- Get medical help if the sick person collapses or if vomiting or diarrhoea is severe.

HYGIENE

Keep your kitchen hygienically clean and safe by observing the following practices.

In the kitchen

- Wash and dry surfaces, sinks and floors regularly using cleaners which incorporate a disinfectant.
- Clean out the refrigerator regularly.
- Never sort out dirty laundry on worktops, even if your kitchen does double as a laundry. If you must, clean the surfaces carefully afterwards with disinfectant.
- Wash your hands between handling different types of food, such as raw and cooked meats, and after handling dirty laundry.
- Try to keep pets out of the kitchen and never allow them to walk or sit on worktops.
- Separate raw and cooked foods in the refrigerator (raw food below cooked food) and don't put anything on a surface that has had raw food on it without first cleaning the area.
- If you can't keep work surfaces scrupulously clean, use chopping boards for preparing food. Plastic ones which can be put in the dishwasher or cleaned with boiling water are more hygienic than wooden ones. Having separate boards for meat, fish and vegetables is a good idea.

- Use clean drying-up cloths each day. It's also a good idea to keep a cloth for heavy drying, such as pots, and one for light drying, such as glasses.
- Mop up spills immediately with paper towels or a clean cloth (see **Marks and spills** section).
- Soak cleaning cloths in a disinfectant solution overnight.
- Keep a lid on the rubbish bin at all times.
- Throw out chipped china and glass, as these can harbour bacteria.
- Keep pet food bowls separate from household crockery and wash them separately. Keep a separate can opener and cutlery for pet food.

With food
- Cook fish, meat and poultry thoroughly before eating.
- When reheating chilled ready meals, make sure they are piping hot (70°C) right through. Check, using a food thermometer inserted in several places.
- Most frozen foods must be completely (not partially) defrosted before cooking. Some frozen foods can be cooked from frozen – see the packet for instructions.
- Food which is to be refrigerated or frozen should be cooled quickly. Place the container in a bowl of iced water to speed this up.
- Use a clean spoon each time you taste food that's cooking.
- Cover food whenever there may be flies around.
- Wash or wipe can lids before you open them; otherwise dust may get into the contents.

KITCHEN SAFETY

Have items you use often within easy reach. Get to things you can't reach using a stepstool or set of kitchen steps. Don't stand on an ordinary chair or stool, the kitchen table or worktops to get at out-of-reach objects.

- Keep knife blades covered when not in use. Store them in a knife block or knife roll or in individual blade cases. *In general*
- Don't let a plug or flex get wet or touch a hot surface.
- Be careful of trailing flexes on small appliances such as kettles. Shorten them if necessary, or use a coiled cable. Don't fill a kettle while it is plugged in.
- Replace damaged flexes.
- Never immerse an electrical appliance in water. If this happens accidentally, let it dry out naturally (which may take as long as 2-3 days at room temperature).
- Mop up spills immediately, especially grease or fat on the floor which could cause you to slip.
- Don't walk on the kitchen floor while it's still wet after washing.
- Use oven gloves when handling hot dishes and pans.
- Keep a small first-aid kit in the kitchen (see page 119) so that you can treat cuts and burns immediately.
- Remember how dangerous the kitchen can be for small children. Fit childproof locks to cupboards and store poisonous and breakable items out of the reach of children.

- Shop for these at the end of a shopping trip. *Perishable*
- Don't leave them to rise in temperature in a *foods* shopping bag or car. If necessary, take a cool box and ice blocks with you.
- Look after your refrigerator. You should keep the temperature between 0°C and 5°C to slow down the rate at which micro-organisms multiply (this won't kill any that are already present).
- Don't put hot food in the fridge; this will raise the overall temperature and enable micro-organisms to multiply more quickly.
- Defrost your fridge regularly if it's not frost free or the automatic defrosting-type, and wash it out with a solution of bicarbonate of soda (15ml to

500ml of warm water). This is usually better than a brand-name cleaner, which may leave a smell of its own.

- Don't open the fridge door more often than necessary.

APPROXIMATE REFRIGERATOR STORAGE TIMES

Raw meat		Cooked meat	
Bacon	7 days	Casseroles/stews	2 days
Bacon (in unopened		Ham	2 days
vacuum pack)	2-3 weeks	Joints	3 days
Fish	should be	Meat pies	2 days
	eaten on day	Sliced meat	2 days
	of purchase		
Joints	3 days	**Dairy produce**	
Minced meat	1 day	Cheese, hard	7-14 days
Offal	1 day	Cheese, semi-hard	7-10 days
Poultry	2 days	Cheese, soft	2-3 days
Raw sliced meats	2 days	Eggs (pointed end	
Sausages	3 days	down)	2 weeks
		Milk (pasteurised,	
Vegetables		homogenised)	4-5 days
Green vegetables	3-4 days		
Salad vegetables	2-3 days		

WHERE TO STORE FOOD

Top and centre shelves
Butter, cheese, convenience foods, cooked items, eggs, lard, margarine, mayonnaise, preserves, salad dressing, sauces, spreads

Lower shelves
Cream, fish, meat (raw meat below cooked meat), milk products, sausages, shellfish

Door
Fruit juice, milk

Salad drawer
Fruit, vegetables

- Transfer ready-frozen foods from the shop to *Frozen foods* your freezer as quickly as possible.
- When freezing food, follow the instructions in the freezer manufacturer's handbook.
- Keep the freezer full if possible to reduce the amount of cold air lost on opening and also reduce condensation. If you're emptying it for defrosting, fill the space with clean towels, plastic bags full of newspapers or bags of ice.

FREEZER STORAGE TIMES

Food	Months	Food	Months
Dairy produce		**Meat and poultry**	
Butter (salted)	3-4	Bacon/ham joints	3-4
Butter (unsalted)	6-8	Beef	12
Cheese (hard)	4-6	Chicken/turkey	10-12
Cheese (soft)	3-4	Cured meat/sliced bacon	2-3
Cream	6-8	Duck/goose	4-6
Ice-cream, mousse, etc.	3-4	Lamb	12
		Minced red meat	3-4
Fish		Offal	2
Fish portions	3-4	Pork	4-6
Oily fish	3-4	Rabbit/hare/game	4-6
Shellfish	2-3	Sausages/sausagemeat	1
White fish	6-8	Veal	4-6
		Venison	10-12
Fruit and vegetables			
Fruit juice	4-6	**Prepared foods**	
Fruit purée	6-8	Boil-in-bag meals	4-6
Fruit (in syrup)	9-12	Bread/bread rolls	2-3
Fruit (without added sugar)	6-8	Cakes	4-6
Vegetables (blanched – most		Ready meals	4-6
varieties)	10-12	if highly seasoned	2-3
		Sandwiches	2-3
		Soups/sauces	3
		Stock	6
		Yeast products/pastries	3-4

Canned foods
- Don't eat foods that are beyond their use-by dates.
- Throw out any cans which are dented, show signs of rust or are 'blown' at the seam (showing signs of swelling). The contents could be damaged.
- Once opened, treat canned food as fresh and store covered in the refrigerator.

Dried foods
- Check best-before date.
- Keep an eye out for weevils (see **Pests** section).
- Don't add new dried goods to half-used quantities you already have.
- Store strongly flavoured dried foods in tightly closed containers to keep them in good condition and prevent their odours transferring to other foods. Buy in small quantities only when needed, as they deteriorate quickly when exposed to air.

FREEZER EMERGENCIES

Power cut
- Leave the freezer shut. Provided it's full, the contents will be fine for up to 24 hours (both upright and chest freezers). To keep the contents as well insulated as possible, cover the freezer with a blanket or rug, making sure you leave the condenser and pipes uncovered.
- If you have to salvage contents, throw out anything such as ice-cream which can't be re-frozen or anything you're worried about (for example, if it smells 'off' or is discoloured, Cook raw ingredients into soups, stews, purées, etc. and refreeze.
- Make sure you have freezer contents insurance. This can usually be arranged on your household insurance.

CULINARY CRISES

If you don't have an asparagus steamer, tie asparagus in bundles and wedge upright in a pan with water coming three-quarters of the way up the stalks. Cover the tips with foil so they can steam.

Asparagus

Prevent your avocado dip or mousse discolouring by putting the stone back into the mixture. Cover it tightly with clingfilm pressed all over the surface. Remember to remove the stone before serving.

Avocado (discoloured)

With kitchen scissors, snip through the rind and fat at 1cm intervals. This also works for steaks.

Bacon rashers (curling)

Whirl it in a blender or mash it through a sieve.

Batter/sauce (lumpy)

Aubergines Slice the aubergines and sprinkle with salt. Leave for 30 minutes, then rinse and pat dry with kitchen paper.
Coffee Don't use boiling water. Allow it to cool for a minute or so before pouring it on to the grounds.

Bitterness

Don't bother to destalk them when freezing. Open freezing is best for fresh fruit. Place them in a single layer on a tray. When frozen, store in an airtight plastic bag or lidded container. Freezing by this method prevents the individual berries or fruits sticking together so that, when thawed, they don't form a pulpy mass and can be used for decoration.

Blackcurrants (freezing)

Put 5ml sugar in the cooking water with cabbage, cauliflower and sprouts.

Brassica (cooking smells)

Stale Run the loaf quickly under the cold tap then heat at 150°C/300°F/gas mark 2 for around 20 minutes. Or wrap it in foil and heat for 10 minutes at 230°C/450°F/gas mark 8 and leave to cool in foil.

Bread

IMPERIAL/METRIC LIQUID CONVERSION CHART

These figures are rounded up or down to give a measurement on both scales.

1 teaspoon	5ml
2 teaspoons	10ml
1 tablespoon	15ml
¼ pint	150ml
½ pint	300ml
1 pint	600ml
1½ pints	900ml
1¾ pints	1 litre

Won't rise Check that the yeast isn't dead by adding a little water and a pinch of sugar, then standing it in the airing cupboard for 15 minutes. If the mixture isn't frothy, it won't work.

Cheese *Dry* Grate, mix with one-third of its weight in butter, a little sherry, brandy or gin, seasoning and some herbs or spice. Put it in a pot and serve as a spread (it will also freeze). Or use dry cheese for toasting.
Stringy Caused by cooking it at too high a temperature.

Chips Dry chipped potatoes thoroughly before cooking to prevent them from splattering.

Coating technique Put seasoned flour in a plastic bag and shake meat or poultry in it to coat without creating a mess.

Crackling Score the rind deeply in a diamond pattern (or get the butcher to do it) and rub with oil and salt to create crisp crackling.

Cream Add a little milk to over-whisked cream. If it doesn't help, abandon it and use to enrich soup, sauces or curries.

MEASURING WITHOUT SCALES

If you're cooking without using weighing scales, the following tablespoon measures are the equivalent of 25g (1oz). Note that they are *level* spoonfuls.

Almonds (ground)	3¾ tbsp
Breadcrumbs (dried)	3¼ tbsp
Breadcrumbs (fresh)	7 tbsp
Butter, lard, margarine	2 tbsp
Cheese (hard, grated)	3 tbsp
Chocolate (grated)	1¼ tbsp
Cocoa	3 tbsp
Coffee (ground)	4 tbsp
Coffee powder (instant)	6½ tbsp
Cornflour, custard powder	2¾ tbsp
Curry powder	3½ tbsp
Desiccated coconut	5 tbsp
Gelatine (powdered)	2 tbsp
Flour (unsifted)	3 tbsp
Ginger (ground)	3½ tbsp
Mustard powder	3½ tbsp
Oatmeal (medium)	2½ tbsp
Rice (uncooked)	1½ tbsp
Salt	1¾ tbsp
Semolina	3 tbsp
Sugar (caster)	2 tbsp
Sugar (granulated)	2 tbsp
Sugar (icing)	2½ tbsp
Sugar (soft brown)	1½ tbsp
Sultanas, currants	2 tbsp
Syrup (unheated)	1 tbsp
Yeast (dried)	1½ tbsp

Curry (too hot) Add any, or a mixture, of the following: lemon juice, milk, a potato, sour cream, plain yoghurt, fromage frais. When eating, take a mouthful of rice or yoghurt, not water.

Eggs *Checking freshness* Put in a bowl of cold water. If fresh, they'll sink; if stale, they'll float. Or break each egg individually in a cup before adding to the other ingredients. An 'off' smell will indicate that the egg is unsuitable for use.

Cracked shells To prevent eggshells from cracking prick them with a pin or special gadget before boiling. Eggs which come straight from the fridge should be put into cold, rather than hot, water.

Curdled (in cream mixture) If curdling occurs when you add eggs to a butter and sugar mixture, add just a little of the weighed-out flour. For easier creaming, warm the bowl first and use room-temperature butter or margarine.

One short Substitute 15ml of vinegar *provided* the recipe uses a raising agent or self-raising flour.

Whites won't whip This is usually due to grease in the bowl or on the whisk, so make sure both are grease-free before use.

Fat (on surface) If there's time, chill and remove fat from the surface of cooked food with a spoon; if not, use sheets of kitchen paper to blot the fat.

Freezer storage Use polythene bags to line rigid containers. Once the contents have frozen a block is formed and the containers can be re-used so you won't need so many.

Garlic breath Eat some parsley or chew coffee beans.

Grapes (peeling) Plunge into hot water a minute or so off the boil, then plunge into cold water. This also works for pickling onions and tomatoes.

Griddle Check whether a griddle is hot enough by sprinkling a little flour on it. If the flour turns brown within three minutes, it's ready.

Honey (hardened) Microwave the honey briefly (having first removed any metal lid) or stand it in a bowl of hot water.

Icing *Crushed* Avoid this by standing the cake on a tin lid and using the body of the tin to cover it. Keep the tin upside down.

Easier Brush the surface of a cake with a little melted jam or sprinkle a small amount of arrowroot over the surface to make icing adhere well.
Hard To soften hard royal icing, add 5ml of glycerine for each 500g of icing sugar.

Add a knob of butter when boiling jam for a set to prevent scum.

Jam (scummy)

Quick-set Melt jelly in a measuring jug with half the specified amount of boiling water. Make up to the full amount with ice cubes.
Won't unmould If jelly or a gelatine mixture won't unmould, run a sharp knife round the top of the mould. Rinse the serving plate with cold water. Stand the mould in a bowl of hot water up to (but not spilling over) the rim. Put the plate over the mould and clamp the two firmly together as you turn them over. Shake gently to release the contents. The wet surface of the serving plate will allow you to slide the jelly into the centre.

Jelly

If you put lettuce or celery into a bowl of cold water it will crisp it up.

Lettuce/celery (floppy)

Take a clean bowl with one egg yolk and *very* gradually beat the curdled mayonnaise into it. This method also works with hollandaise sauce. Note that the mayonnaise is less likely to curdle if all the ingredients are at room temperature.

Mayonnaise (separating)

Tough or rubbery mince (or other meat) can be avoided by not adding salt to it before cooking.

Mince (tough)

To prevent pasta from sticking together, add 15ml of oil to the cooking water and stir only occasionally.

Pasta (sticking)

After making pastry, let it rest in the refrigerator for 30 minutes before you roll it out.

Pastry (shrinking)

Profiteroles
(heavy)   You *must* pierce these and all choux pastry products the minute they come out of the oven to reduce the steam.

Salt (damp)   Put a few grains of rice in the container or salt cellar.

Saltiness   *Anchovies*   Soak anchovies in milk for 30 minutes before use.

Bacon/gammon   If there's no time to soak a joint, put it in a pan of cold water and bring to the boil. Pour the water away and simmer, following cooking instructions, in fresh water.

Soup   Add some extra grated or diced vegetables or some rice or pasta to absorb some of the salt. Or add a couple of quartered potatoes and remove before serving. If you've time, make up a fresh, unseasoned batch of soup and mix the two together. Half the mixture may then be frozen (if suitable) or used as a base for a sauce. If desperate, put ½ pint (300ml) of milk into a clean pan. In a bowl, knead together 1oz (30g) of unsalted butter with 1 tbsp (15ml) of flour. Boil up the milk and whisk in tiny pieces of the butter and flour mixture until it thickens. This can then be added gradually to the oversalted soup until the right flavour balance is reached.

Sauce   *To thicken*   If a sauce, gravy or casserole isn't thick enough, mix a little cornflour with water or some of the liquid. Pour a little of the sauce on to the cornflour and mix well. Add to the dish and continue to cook.

To prevent a skin   Cover with a piece of greaseproof paper smoothed out well. With a sweet sauce, leave out some of the sugar when making it and spread it in a thin layer on top. Stir it in before serving.

Sausages
(slippery)   Sausages will turn more easily if you anchor them together in pairs with cocktail sticks. Leave a space between them to ensure they cook all over.

OVEN TEMPERATURES

While most modern recipe books spell out oven temperatures, some older ones use words. Here's what they mean.

Very cool	110°C/225°F/gas mark ¼
	120°C/250°F/gas mark ½
Cool	140°C/275°F/gas mark 1
	150°C/300°F/gas mark 2
Moderate	160°C/325°F/gas mark 3
	180°C/350°F/gas mark 4
Moderately hot	190°C/375°F/gas mark 5
Fairly hot	200°C/400°F/gas mark 6
Hot	220°C/425°F/gas mark 7
	230°C/450°F/gas mark 8
Very hot	240°C/475°F/gas mark 9

Self-raising flour

If you have no self-raising flour, add 12½ml of baking powder to each 225g of plain flour. Sift well.

Skinning

Fish Dip your fingers in salt to give a firm grasp. Also, when gutting a fish, if you pour plenty of salt into the body cavity it will help you to remove the insides.
Peppers Put under a hot grill or hold (on a fork) over a gas flame until charred all over. Plunge into cold water then rub off the skins. Or, after removing from the grill, leave to cool in a plastic bag or covered bowl until the skins peel off, which also collects the juices.

Sogginess

Biscuits Put a couple of sugar lumps in the biscuit tin to absorb moisture.
Salad Don't dress your salad until just before eating. The quick and easy way to organise salad is

to make the dressing in the salad bowl, pile the salad on top and toss the ingredients together at the last minute. Or keep the salad dressing in a separate jug and allow guests to pour it on for themselves.

Sticky foods *(cutting)* Dip kitchen scissor blades into hot water or flour when cutting up sticky foods such as dates and dried apricots.

Tomatoes *(green)* Ripen in a warm dark place with a ripe tomato or banana skin among them.

MICROWAVE COOKING

Microwave cooking is a special technique; the handbook supplied with your microwave should explain how to do it. However, there are some problem foods which will never cook well in a standard microwave. Obviously, if you have a combination model or one with a grill or browning element, some of the following items will cook satisfactorily. Problematic foods are:

- eggs in shells
- eggs out of shells, unless you have first pricked the membrane which covers the yolk
- batters, bread, meringues, pizzas, roast potatoes, soufflés
- large cakes
- anything you want to brown.

NEVER PUT ANYTHING METALLIC INTO A MICROWAVE.

Marks and spills

- Basic stain removal kit • Safety
  - Treatment tips • Food stains
    - Other stains

The sad fact of life is that virtually all everyday activities – eating, drinking, chores and leisure pastimes – offer possibilities for creating stains in a matter of seconds; getting rid of them takes longer, but most stains respond to a basic battery of chemicals and it is worth building up a kit specifically for stain removal, and keeping it somewhere safe and out of reach of children (many of the products are poisonous). Spills and marks are best treated when fresh.

Don't rely on the fact that you've probably got hydrogen peroxide in the medicine cupboard or white vinegar in the larder. Keep a small bottle of each in your stain removal kit as well.

BASIC STAIN REMOVAL KIT

Acetone (non-oily nail varnish remover)
Flammable. Do not inhale. Do not use on acetate or tri-acetate.

Ammonia
Always use diluted in a solution of one part ammonia to four parts water. It gives off fumes, so ventilate the room well. Keep out of eyes and away from skin or fabric. Rinse well with cold water if you do get it on any of these. Do not use on wool or silk.

Biological (enzyme) detergent
Follow manufacturer's instructions. Always soak whole item since slight colour change may occur. Do not use on wool, silk, non-colourfast fabrics, flame-resistant and rubberised fabrics. Do not soak items with metal fastenings.

Bleach
Dilute according to manufacturer's instructions. Do not use on non-colourfast fabrics, drip-dry fabrics, crease-resistant fabrics, embossed or piqué fabrics, silk or wool. Take care not to spill it on your clothes.

French chalk (or fuller's earth or talcum powder)
Sprinkle an even layer over the stain and brush off the chalk when it becomes impregnated.

Glycerine
Dilute in a solution of one part glycerine to one part warm water.

Grease solvents
They come in aerosol, liquid and stick forms. Follow manufacturer's instructions for use, especially with aerosols, which can produce ring marks if sprayed too close to a stain. Repeat the application as necessary, leaving the final layer on for several hours.

Hydrogen peroxide
Buy in 20-volume strength and dilute one part hydrogen peroxide to six parts cold water. Always soak the whole item since the solution has a bleaching effect. Do not use on nylon or flame-resistant fabrics.

Laundry borax
Available from chemists. Dilute 15ml laundry borax with 500ml warm water for sponging and soaking. Immerse whole item when soaking, as slight bleaching may occur. Do not soak for more than 15 minutes.
White fabrics can be stretched over a bowl or basin and the dampened stain sprinkled with borax powder, then rinsed in hot water.

Methylated spirit
Flammable, poisonous and smells strongly. Use neat, but test first as it may affect colour. Do not use on acetate, tri-acetate or French-polished surfaces.

Pre-wash laundry products
Useful for treating stains on washable fabrics. Follow manufacturer's instructions.

Proprietary stain removers
Use these according to your household needs. Look for them in hardware shops, d-i-y stores, department stores and chemists. They will be sold as removers of specific stains, such as adhesives, chewing-gum, ink, tar and so on.

Surgical spirit
Buy as an alternative to methylated spirit.

White spirit (paint thinner)
Flammable. Do not inhale. Do not use on acetate, tri-acetate.

White vinegar (dilute acetic acid)
Do not use on acetate or tri-acetate.

Don't decant stain removal products into new containers unless you mark them clearly with firmly stuck labels detailing both the product and instructions for its use.

SAFETY

These are some rules which you should always follow.

- Work in a well-ventilated area so that you're not affected by fumes from the chemicals.
- Wear gloves to protect your hands.
- Don't let chemicals get in your eyes or on your skin or clothes (wear a plastic apron). If your eyes or skin are affected, rinse thoroughly with cold water and, if stinging or burning persists, call your GP or go to a hospital Accident and Emergency department.
- Don't smoke when using chemicals and don't use them near a naked flame.
- Keep children and pets out of the way. Be particularly careful with ventilation in the vicinity of 'fixed' pets, such as caged birds.

TREATMENT TIPS

- Keep a file with care labels for things like upholstery, curtain fabrics, carpets and any item that has no instructions sewn into it.
- Follow instructions to the letter. Don't make up a chemical solution that is stronger than recommended and don't assume that what worked on fabric 'A' will automatically work on fabric 'B'.
- Don't mix treatments.
- Act as soon as you find a stain. Fresh marks are easier to treat than those that have set. Blot (with white absorbent paper or towel) or scrape up (with the back of a knife blade or a spoon) as much as possible before starting treatment. When blotting or scraping, take care not to spread the stain. Work from the outside to the centre.
- ALWAYS TEST any treatment on an inconspicuous part of the stained item. Apply to seams of garments, underside of furniture, and so on. Leave for long enough to check any reaction.
- Go to a professional cleaner if (a) the manufacturer recommends this; (b) you don't feel able to tackle the stain (too big, mystery substance . . .) yourself; and (c) if you've tried treatment and it hasn't worked. In this case, be sure to tell the cleaner what was spilt and, where appropriate, what you've already tried on it.

FOOD AND DRINK STAINS

Beer

First, try warm water on *carpets* and *washable fabrics*. A squirt from a soda syphon often works on carpets; then blot as dry as possible and, if marking persists, use a solution of carpet shampoo. (Note: this and any other stain removed by carpet shampoo may produce an unnaturally clean area which requires you to shampoo the whole carpet to even up the colour.)

Dried beer Remove from *carpets* with methylated spirit; and from *washable fabrics* (after laundering) with a hydrogen peroxide solution (one part 20-volume strength hydrogen peroxide to six parts cold water). *Coloured fabrics* should be sponged with a white vinegar solution (30ml white vinegar to 500ml cold water), then washed as usual. On *non-washable fabrics*, sponge with warm water, then white vinegar solution or apply an aerosol dry cleaner.

If you intend to use a chemical-based cleaning product on a foam-backed carpet, *always* check first with the manufacturer.

Beetroot

Rinse *washable* fabrics in cold water, then wash in a biological detergent solution. Alternatively, stretch white fabrics over a bowl and sprinkle laundry borax on the stain before rinsing with hot water and laundering. *Coloured fabrics* can be soaked in a warm solution of laundry borax (15ml laundry borax to 500ml water).

Check **Basic stain removal kit** (pages 25-7) before embarking on any remedy to see if the material you propose to work on will stand up to the treatment.

Chewing-gum   On *carpets* and *upholstery*, use a proprietary chewing-gum remover. Place marked clothes in a fridge or freezer to harden the gum and then pick off as much as possible. Launder *washable fabrics*; use a liquid stain remover followed by sponging on *non-washable fabrics*.

Chocolate   Scrape off as much as possible. Launder *washable fabrics* in a biological detergent solution. Use a stain remover or carpet/upholstery shampoo on *carpets* and *non-washable fabrics*.

Coffee   Blot well. Spray *carpets* with a soda syphon or sponge with warm water, then pat dry. If necessary, use a proprietary stain remover. Soak *washable fabrics* in a biological detergent solution and launder. Remove traces with a proprietary stain remover or bleach (only on suitable white fabrics). Treat *non-washable fabrics* with a laundry borax solution (15ml laundry borax to 500ml warm water), rinse by sponging with clear water and pat dry. Clear any residual marks with a proprietary stain remover.

Curry   This can be difficult to remove. Have bad marks and marks on expensive items removed professionally. Otherwise, scrape up as much as possible before treatment. Sponge *carpets* with a laundry borax solution (15ml laundry borax to 500ml warm water) or apply a stain remover. Sponge with clean water and pat dry. Soak *washable fabrics* in warm water, then rub in a glycerine solution (one part glycerine to one part warm water) and leave for an hour. Rinse with clear water. Re-apply if necessary. Launder using biological detergent. Bleach can be used on suitable white fabrics. On *non-washable fabrics* use a laundry borax solution (15ml laundry borax to 500ml warm water) and sponge clean.

Egg   Scrape up as much cooked egg as possible, rubbing gently with a dry cloth to loosen the stain. On *carpets*, use a proprietary stain remover/carpet spotting kit followed by an application of carpet shampoo. On *non-washable fabrics*, sponge lightly with cold salty water, then with clear water. If the mark persists, use upholstery shampoo or a proprietary stain remover. Use salt water on *washable fabrics*, then rinse. Soak, then launder in biological detergent.

Fruit juice

Blot quickly with kitchen paper or a white towel. On *carpets*, sponge with warm water, then use a carpet shampoo. Any remaining colour should be dabbed with methylated spirit. On *washable fabrics*, rinse in cold running water. Table and bed linen should then be stretched over a bowl or basin and hot water poured through the stain. Remaining marks should be covered with a glycerine solution (one part glycerine to one part warm water) and the items then laundered as usual. Other washable fabrics should be soaked, then laundered with a heavy-duty detergent. On *non-washable fabrics*, sponge with cold water and use a proprietary stain remover.

Ice-cream

Scrape up as much as possible. On *carpets*, wipe with a damp cloth and apply carpet shampoo or a carpet spotting kit. Use a proprietary stain remover on any remaining grease, first checking – where appropriate – that the product is safe on a foam-backed carpet. On *non-washable fabrics*, use a proprietary stain remover and bleach out any traces of colour with a solution of hydrogen peroxide (one part 20-volume strength hydrogen peroxide to six parts cold water). Soak *washable fabrics* in a warm biological detergent solution (or ordinary detergent if the fabric is not suitable). Launder at the highest

Check **Basic stain removal kit** (pages 25-7) before embarking on any remedy to see if the material you propose to work on will stand up to the treatment.

31

temperature the fabric can take. Fabrics such as *silk* and *wool*, which can't be soaked, should be sponged with a warm solution of laundry borax (15ml laundry borax to 500ml water), then clean water.

Jam/preserves   Scrape up as much as possible. Wipe *carpets* with a damp cloth, then use a carpet shampoo. Remove any colour with methylated spirit. On *non-washable fabrics*, sponge with a warm solution of washing-up liquid, blot and repeat if necessary. Rinse with clean water. Bad marks may need to be covered with laundry borax powder for 15 minutes, then sponged. Alternatively, use a proprietary stain remover. Most stains come out when laundering *washable fabrics*. If not, soak in a laundry borax solution (15ml laundry borax to 500ml warm water), then re-launder.

Milk   Treat carpets and non-washable fabrics immediately to prevent an almost ineradicable smell. On *carpets*, squirt with a soda syphon, blot well and use a carpet spotting kit. Sponge *non-washable fabrics* with clear warm water and blot. Use a stain remover or upholstery spotting kit. Rinse, then launder *washable* fabrics, and soak remaining stains in biological detergent.

Oil, fat, grease   Scrape and wipe up as much as possible. On *carpets*, it helps to use white blotting paper or brown paper and a medium-hot iron to absorb as much grease as possible. Take care on foam-backed carpets not to damage the backing. Whisk up a solution of dry foam carpet shampoo and use the lather to treat the marks, repeating until they disappear. Even when you think you've cleared a stain it may return later as it works its way up the pile, in which case repeat the treatment. On *non-washable fabrics*, sprinkle a layer of talcum powder. As it absorbs the grease, wipe it off with kitchen paper and apply another layer. Leave the final layer for several hours, then brush off. Alternatively, on suitable fabrics, use the blotting paper/brown paper and iron treatment followed by a stain remover. On *washable fabrics*, launder in the hottest water possible. On fabrics which can take only warm water, use a stain remover, then wash. On *delicate fabrics* and *wool*, dab with eucalyptus oil, then sponge or launder.

Tea

On *carpets*, mop us as much as possible. Squirt with a soda syphon, blot and, when dry, apply a stain remover. If the tea contained milk, use carpet shampoo to remove the grease. On *non-washable fabrics*, use a laundry borax solution (15ml laundry borax to 500ml warm water), then rinse. When dry, use a stain remover or upholstery spotting kit. On *washable fabrics*, rinse out as much as possible in warm water, then soak in biological detergent before laundering.

Wine (any colour)

On *carpets*, squirt with a soda syphon and pat dry. Use repeated applications of carpet shampoo solution until clean. Rinse with cold water and blot dry. On *non-washable fabrics*, blot with white kitchen paper and sponge with warm water. If marks remain, sprinkle with talcum powder while still damp and brush it off after five minutes. Repeat until mark disappears.
Stretch *washable fabrics* over a bowl or basin and pour hot water through the stain. Soak in a solution of laundry borax (15ml laundry borax to 500ml warm water). Launder as usual. Use a solution of bleach on suitable fabrics where a stain remains.

Check **Basic stain removal kit** (pages 25-7) before embarking on any remedy to see if the material you propose to work on will stand up to the treatment.

OTHER STAINS

Adhesives   Most adhesive manufacturers produce solvents for their products; some are available over the counter, while for others you have to contact the manufacturer directly. If you think there's a risk of spillage, buy the solvent before you use the adhesive. In any event, quickly scrape up as much of the spill as possible. If the adhesive has set on to the carpet, trim the pile with very sharp scissors.

> If you intend to use a chemical-based cleaning product on a foam-backed carpet, *always* check first with the manufacturer.

Clear adhesive   Use acetone (non-oily nail varnish remover) on *carpets* and *fabrics*.
Epoxy resin   Use cellulose thinners on *carpets* and *fabrics*.
Latex adhesive   Use liquid grease solvent on *carpets* and *fabrics*. On *hard surfaces*, wait until the adhesive has just set and rub with a finger.
Sticky label residue   Use white spirit, methylated spirit or cellulose thinners on *hard surfaces* other than metals; on *metals*, use amyl acetate or nail varnish remover. Use a proprietary chewing-gum remover on *fabrics*.

Baths   (See also **Bathrooms and showers** section.)
Vitreous enamel/porcelain baths   On *drip stains*, use a cleaner approved by the Vitreous Enamel Development Council (VEDC) – see **Addresses**. On *hard water marks*, use a scale remover. On *tidemarks*, use a cloth dampened with white spirit.
Plastic baths   Follow the manufacturer's instructions regarding cleaning. Scratches can be removed by rubbing lightly with metal cream polish.

After you have scraped off as much as possible, sponge with warm water or laundry borax solution, which should remove marks from *carpets* and *washable fabrics*. Bad stains on carpets will respond to a solution of laundry borax (15ml laundry borax to 500ml warm water) or a proprietary stain remover. Use an aerosol stain remover on *non-washable fabrics* and *upholstery*. Droppings on washing hung out to dry should come out with a further laundering. Those which contain the stain of berries can be treated with a hydrogen peroxide solution (one part 20-volume strength hydrogen peroxide to six parts cold water) or diluted bleach (white fabrics only).

Bird droppings

Soak *washable fabrics* in cold salty water, then in biological detergent solution made up to the manufacturer's instructions. Launder as usual. Sponge *non-washable fabrics* with a solution of ammonia (2.5ml ammonia to 1 litre cold water). Rinse with cold water and pat dry with kitchen paper. Squirt *carpets* with a soda syphon, then sponge with cold water. Do not add salt to the water as this creates permanent dampness which will attract dirt to the spot. Prop a *mattress* on its side so it doesn't get too wet and apply a thick paste of bicarbonate of soda mixed with as little water as possible. When this dries, brush it off and re-apply if necessary. Then sponge with cold salty water.

Blood

Scrape up as much as possible using a spoon or fingernail. (On *hard surfaces*, first harden the wax by holding a plastic bag of ice cubes on it so it chips off more easily.) Use a medium-hot iron applied over white blotting paper or brown parcel paper to

Candle wax

Check **Basic stain removal kit** (pages 25-7) before embarking on any remedy to see if the material you propose to work on will stand up to the treatment.

absorb as much of the wax residue as possible (use the iron on a low setting for delicate fabrics such as Dralon). Remove any traces of colour with methylated spirit on *carpets*, and a proprietary stain remover on *washable* and *non-washable fabrics* and *wall coverings*.

Running colours   To remove the dye from *machine-washable* garments which have been put in a washing-machine with an item that has run, use a special dye remover. Otherwise, use bleach (on suitable white fabrics) or soak in a biological detergent solution.

Cosmetics   *Make-up*   Remove foundation cream, lipstick and mascara with white spirit or a proprietary stain remover. Follow by laundering *washable fabrics* or by sponging *non-washable fabrics* with warm water.
Nail varnish   Spilt nail varnish should be blotted immediately to stop the stain spreading. Remove with oily nail varnish remover.

Flowers   Launder *washable fabrics* and treat remaining marks with methylated spirit, then rinse. To remove stains in *vases* and other containers, soak in cold water with 15ml of household bleach. Marks on *wallcoverings* should be scraped gently with a fingernail, then cleaned with a proprietary stain remover for non-washable coverings or with a solution of washing-up liquid for washable coverings.

Grass   On *washable fabrics*, stains should come out in the wash. Otherwise, use methylated spirit and rinse. On *non-washable* cricket flannels, cover the stain with cream of tartar powder and fine salt (mixed in equal parts), leave on for 15 minutes and brush dry. Dry clean as usual.

Inks   *Ballpoints*   Ballpoint ink is difficult to remove. On *carpets*, dry up as much as possible with cotton wool balls, cotton buds or a paper towel. Dab with methylated spirit or use a proprietary stain remover.

If you are unsuccessful, get in touch with the pen manufacturer for help. On *vinyl bedheads, wallcoverings* and other products, act quickly. Scrub briskly with a nailbrush dipped into a solution of washing-up liquid.

Felt-tips Ink stains should be removed with cotton wool or a paper towel, then dabbed with methylated spirit. *Washable fabrics* can be laundered; *non-washable fabrics* treated with a proprietary stain remover. Use a non-abrasive household cleaner or methylated spirit on *vinyl products*. Sponge with a solution of washing-up liquid and restore the finish with an application of vinyl or upholstery cleaner.

Fountain pens On *carpets*, squirt with a soda syphon to dilute the stain and blot up as much as possible. Make up a hot solution of soapflakes and apply as a poultice on a white pad. Leave for at least 15 minutes. Blot and repeat until the marks go. Rinse with clear water. Bad marking may need treatment with a carpet spotting kit and possibly a carpet shampoo. Don't let the stain dry on fabrics before treatment; use cold water to keep it damp. Launder *washable fabrics*, bleaching white ones if necessary. On *non-washable fabrics*, use a proprietary stain remover.

Iron mould

On *washable fabrics*, squirt with lemon juice (bottled is fine) and cover with a thin layer of salt for an hour. Rinse and wash as usual. On *non-washable fabrics*, use a stain remover.

Mildew

On *non-washable fabrics*, brush well, outdoors if possible, to get rid of the spores. If suitable, dab with hydrogen peroxide solution (one part 20-

Check **Basic stain removal kit** (pages 25-7) before embarking on any remedy to see if the material you propose to work on will stand up to the treatment.

volume strength hydrogen peroxide to six parts cold water) and rinse with clear water. Launder *washable fabrics*, then treat remaining marks with a hydrogen peroxide solution (or household bleach solution on white fabrics). Repeated laundering will remove most marks, and proprietary stain removers are available.

Mildew on *leather* should be sponged with a disinfectant solution (5ml disinfectant to 500ml warm water) or wiped with neat antiseptic mouthwash. Apply hide food or shoe polish, depending upon the item.

Mildew on *plastic* shower curtains should be sponged with a mild solution of household bleach. Rinse and apply a detergent solution (or launder if suitable). A proprietary bactericide of the kind usually applied before hanging wallpaper will reduce regrowth.

Mud   Allow to dry, then brush off as much as possible using a stiff hand brush or vacuum cleaner tool. On *carpets*, use a carpet spotting kit followed by methylated spirit on any traces of colour. On *non-washable fabrics*, sponge with a warm solution of washing-up liquid, rinse with clear water and blot well. Laundering removes most mud from *washable fabrics* but bad marks should first be treated with a stain remover.

Paints   *Emulsion and other water-based paint*   Comes off most things if you blot them well, then sponge with cold water and launder appropriately. Treat immediately.

Gloss and other oil-based paint   Spoon up as much as possible and dab the residue with white spirit or a stain remover. Rinse with clean water and repeat treatment until marks are cleared. Launder *washable fabrics*; shampoo *carpet* and *upholstery*.

Urine and vomit are hazards to be expected of pets that don't live in cages or hutches. Buy a proprietary pet stain remover, which will both remove marks and deodorise the area. See also **Urine** and **Vomit** on pages 40-1.

Pet stains

Slight scorch marks on pile *carpets* are best removed by carefully trimming the pile with sharp scissors. Treat worse marks by brushing vigorously to get rid of damaged fibres, then rub gently with coarse glasspaper until the area is clean.
For very bad scorch marks you may need to call in a carpet restorer to replace a patch or follow the instruction on **Replacing damaged carpet** in the **Household and cleaning problems** section. On *washable fabrics*, apply a glycerine solution (equal parts glycerine and warm water) for an hour or so, then sponge with warm water. Treat bad marks by sponging with a laundry borax solution (15ml laundry borax to 500ml warm water). Rinse with warm water and repeat as necessary. On *washable fabrics*, rub the area under cold running water, then soak in a laundry borax solution. Launder as usual. You can use a hydrogen peroxide solution (one part 20-volume strength hydrogen peroxide to six parts cold water) to bleach some fabrics.

Scorch marks

Scrape up as much as possible. Apply methylated spirit or a stain remover to remaining marks on *carpets* and *non-washable fabrics*, then carpet/upholstery shampoo. On *washable fabrics*, use a stain remover or white spirit before laundering as usual.

Shoe polish

Check **Basic stain removal kit** (pages 25-7) before embarking on any remedy to see if the material you propose to work on will stand up to the treatment.

Tar   Scrape gently to remove as much as possible without damaging carpet or fabric. On *carpets* and *non-washable fabrics*, apply a glycerine solution (equal parts glycerine and water) for an hour, then rinse with clean water. Use a carpet spotting kit or stain remover, then rinse with cold water. On *washable fabrics*, place an absorbent pad of paper or towel on top of the mark and apply eucalyptus oil on a cotton wool pad from below. Wash.

Urine   On *carpets*, use a special cleaner which contains a deodorant. Otherwise, squirt with a soda syphon, blot well and rinse two or three times with cold water to which you have added a few drops of antiseptic. On *non-washable fabrics*, first sponge with cold water, then pat dry. Re-sponge with a solution of 15ml white vinegar to 500ml warm water, repeating if necessary. Rinse with clear water. Rinse *washable fabrics* in cold water, then launder. Use a hydrogen peroxide solution (one part 20-volume strength hydrogen peroxide to six parts cold water) to bleach remaining stains on suitable white fabrics.

On *carpets*, scrape up as much as possible. Squirt   ***Vomit***
with a soda syphon and blot. Sponge gently with a
solution of laundry borax (15ml laundry borax to
500ml warm water) or the lather from a solution of
carpet shampoo. Repeat until the mark disappears.
Rinse with warm water containing a few drops of
antiseptic.

Treat *mattresses* as for carpets, using upholstery
rather than carpet shampoo. Prop the mattress on
its side during treatment to prevent absorption of
liquid and allow to dry naturally before sleeping on
it. *Non-washable fabrics* should have the deposit
removed, then be dry-cleaned or sponged with
warm water containing a few drops of ammonia. If
suitable, use an upholstery shampoo. On *washable
fabrics*, remove deposit and rinse under a cold water
tap. Use an enzyme detergent on fabrics which can
take it or launder according to the manufacturer's
instructions.

Household and cleaning problems

- Bathrooms and showers   • Beds and bedrooms
- Blinds   • Carpets and rugs   • Ceramic tiles
- China, earthenware and porcelain   • Clothes
- Curtains and rails   • Electrical appliances
- Fireplaces   • Floorings   • Furniture
- Gas cookers   • Glass   • Jewellery
- Kitchen equipment   • Metals   • Miscellaneous
- Paintwork   • Plastics   • Saucepans/cookware

H ousework chores never seem to go away – though you can often save yourself time by doing things the right way the first time.

BATHROOMS AND SHOWERS

Mildew   *On shower curtains*   Soak the curtains in a solution of one part household bleach to four parts water. Rinse, and then hand or machine wash according to care instructions.

Steamy bathroom   To help prevent a bathroom from steaming up, run some cold water into the bath before adding the hot.

Tidemarks   *On plastic baths*   These respond to a little metal polish applied on a soft cloth.
On vitreous/porcelain enamelled baths   Apply   white spirit and wash and rinse off thoroughly.

Cleaning discoloured grouting Use an old clean **Tiles** toothbrush and a solution of one part household bleach to six parts of cold water to clean the grouting. Rinse and dry. Avoid getting splashes on the carpet or on clothes.

Cleaning off soap splashes Clean with a solution of one part white vinegar to four parts water. Rinse and dry.

BEDS AND BEDROOMS

Most blankets, pillows and man-made fibre duvets **Bedding** are too heavy to wash in a domestic washing-machine. Take them to a launderette, where the machine capacity is larger and where often there is a centrifugal spinner which will get them dry more quickly.

Use an extra-low voltage electric underblanket **Cold bed** which can be left on all night if necessary.

Assembly Turn the cover inside out. Put both **Duvets** hands into the top corners of the cover and take hold of two corners of the duvet. Shake vigorously until everything is in position. Double and king-size duvet covers are best done by two people.

Cleaning and care
- Always use a duvet cover to prevent a duvet from getting dirty. Some duvets can be washed; those that can't should be cleaned by a specialist firm. Don't use a coin-operated cleaning machine, since toxic fumes may linger in the filling.
- Shake duvets regularly to keep the filling evenly distributed. Hang over a washing-line in the fresh air from time to time.

Pillows   Both foam- and natural-filled pillows can be washed out but when wet may be too heavy for a domestic washing-machine. Go to a launderette (see **Bedding** above).
If you hand wash a pillow, squeeze it well to get rid of as much moisture as possible, then peg it on a washing-line. It may take several days to dry.

BLINDS

Festoon   Vacuum with the upholstery tool. From time to time, dismantle and wash or dry-clean.

Roller   *If dirty*   Vacuum with the upholstery tool or use a soft brush. If spongeable, use a solution of upholstery cleaner (follow the manufacturer's instructions). Rehang while still damp.
If it refuses to wind   Re-tension by pulling down the blind halfway. Remove from brackets and roll up by hand. Pull down to check tension. If not satisfactory, repeat the process.

Venetian   If you don't have a special cleaning brush, wear thick cotton gloves and run your hands along both sides of the slats. If you need to wash the blind, line the bath with a towel to prevent scratching the surface, and avoid immersing the operating mechanism.

CARPETS AND RUGS

Creeping rugs   Use double-sided tape to fix a rug to a hard floor. You can buy special products to keep a rug in place on a carpet.

You have, of course, saved an offcut of carpet from the time it was laid!

Damaged carpet

- Cut out a square of thick cardboard slightly larger than the patch that needs mending.
- Lay it over the damaged patch and, with a sharp knife, cut round the edge.
- Place the cardboard on your offcut, lining up pattern and pile direction, and cut out the shape.
- Line the edge of the hole with double-sided tape.
- Press the patch into position, smoothing the pile to conceal the edges.

Avoid furniture marks by:

Marks on carpet

- using castor cups under feet
- moving furniture around regularly
- damping indentations and using the vacuum cleaner nozzle attachment to raise the pile.

Also, get everyone to wear slippers or go barefoot around the home.

It's the same with new mattresses on old bed bases: the new picks up the indentations of the old. So always buy new underlay to accompany a new carpet.

New carpet, old underlay?

Burnt With a sharp nail or embroidery scissors, trim off the bits or tips of the pile. (Badly burnt patches will need replacing – see **Damaged carpet** above.)

Pile

Crushed Dampen a piece of cotton cloth and put it over the crushed area. Gently apply an iron, as hot as the carpet fibre can stand. (Test this on your offcut of carpet before starting.) When dry, brush with a hand brush to raise the pile.

Caused by overwetting when shampooing. Have the carpet re-stretched professionally.

Rippled carpets

When having stair carpet laid, insist on the provision of extra length so that you can move the carpet when wear starts to show on the 'nosings' (the bits on the bends). This extra is usually stored at the bottom of the stairs.

Stair carpet wear

- With a tack remover, take out the carpet tacks.
- Check the condition of the underlay and replace worn sections.
- Using the spare length, move the carpet up the stairs and re-tack.
- A stair carpet held by rods is easily moved. Slide out the rods, move the carpet and replace.
- A stair carpet held by grips should be moved in the same way (after easing it off the grips).

CERAMIC TILES

Broken   For a single broken tile:
- remove the grouting surrounding the damaged tile with a pointed scraper;
- chip out the tile with a hammer and chisel;
- scrape out the old adhesive and sand the recessed area smooth;
- apply new tile adhesive and the new tile;
- regrout around it (and you'll probably need to clean all the other grouting so it doesn't stand out).

CHINA, EARTHENWARE AND PORCELAIN

Bone china   Wash by hand, taking care not to knock pieces together and chip them. Some bone china is dishwasher safe.
Don't wash china with gold or silver decoration in a dishwasher; it will gradually come off. Clean off persistent marks by rubbing with salt, not a scouring pad.

Wash according to instructions, handling carefully as earthenware is easily chipped and broken. Before cooking with earthenware, check whether it is safe to use in a hot oven . *Earthenware*

Always wash porcelain articles by hand, never in a dishwasher. Vases and figurines that are cracked and chipped should not be immersed in water, just sponged with a damp cloth. *Porcelain*

> Don't cook with or eat out of a chipped or cracked piece of china or glass; the cracks harbour germs.

CLOTHES

Use a defuzzing gadget or sticky tape to remove fluff from jumpers. *Bobbly jumpers*

Stick small pieces of foam rubber or wind rubber bands on the end of wooden hangers to stop clothes falling off. *Coat hangers*

When removing clothes from a tumble-dryer, put them on hangers immediately to eliminate the need for ironing. If there is no iron handy, hang a creased garment in the bathroom and create as much steam as possible. *Creasing crises*

If you perspire heavily, stitch underarm shields into your clothes. *Perspiration problems*

Leave wet and dirty raincoats to dry before brushing off marks and mud. *Raincoats*

47

LAUNDRY CODE SYMBOLS

wording on label	washing temperature	
	machine	hand
'wash in cotton cycle/ programme' or 'wash as cotton'	very hot 95°C	hand hot 50°C
	normal action, rinse and spin	
'wash in cotton cycle/ programme' or 'wash as cotton'	hot 60°C	hand hot 50°C
	normal action, rinse and spin	
'wash in synthetics cycle/ programme' or 'wash as synthetics'		hand hot 50°C
	reduced action, cold rinse, reduced spin or drip dry	
'wash in cotton cycle/ programme' or 'wash as cotton'		warm 40°C
	normal action, rinse and spin	
'wash in synthetics cycle/ programme' or 'wash as synthetics'		warm 40°C
	reduced action, cold rinse, reduced spin	
'wash in wool cycle/programme' or 'wash as wool'		warm 40°C
	much reduced action, normal rinse and spin (don't hand wring)	
hand wash	see garment label	
do not wash		

may be chlorine bleached

do not chlorine bleach

tumble dry

do not tumble dry

hot iron (cotton, linen, viscose)

warm iron (polyester mixtures, wool)

cool iron (acetate, acrylic, nylon, polyester, tri-acetate)

do not iron

dry-clean (in all solvents)

dry-clean (suitable for dry cleaning with certain solvents and by certain procedures only. Seek the advice of a specialist dry-cleaning firm)

do not dry-clean

Use dry hair shampoo on the wool lining of a sheepskin coat.

Sheepskin

An open container of bicarbonate of soda will absorb smells.

Smelly wardrobes

Mend clothes before wearing them. Safety pins and other d-i-y mending implements cause damage and spoil the appearance of clothes (see also **Sewing and mending tips** section).

Wear and tear

Rub soap on zips so that they run smoothly. Wipe them with a tissue to prevent residue getting on the fabric (see also **Sewing and mending tips** section).

Zips

CURTAINS AND RAILS

Dust with the suction nozzle of a vacuum cleaner. While curtains are being cleaned, take the rails down and, if plastic, wash them with a solution of washing-up liquid, using an old clean toothbrush to get into the channels. Put the rails in the bath if possible. Wooden and metal curtain rails and poles should be dusted and a thin layer of appropriate polish applied, buffed off well so it won't get on the curtain fabric.
Sticking curtain gliders Spray with an aerosol lubricant before rehanging the curtains.

Curtain rails

It is best to have curtains dry-cleaned professionally, using a specialist curtain cleaner if they are made of expensive material. A specialist will come to your home, measure the curtains and clean and rehang them, ensuring that the correct length and width is maintained. Don't use a coin-operated cleaning machine unless you are sure that the solvent is fresh. It can harbour body odours which can be transferred to the curtain fabric. Even

Curtains

curtains made from washable fabrics are best dry-cleaned, especially if they are lined, since the two fabrics might shrink at different rates and cause puckering. Also, large curtains are too heavy for a domestic washing-machine, and create wet bulk that is difficult to dry if washed by hand in a bath.

Keep curtains clean between professional cleanings by using the upholstery tool on the vacuum cleaner to remove dust. If they are not too large and heavy, hang the curtains in the fresh air from time to time.

Nets Net curtains should be washed frequently before they start to look dirty, otherwise they won't come clean. Soiled net curtains may benefit from being treated with a proprietary whitener.

ELECTRICAL APPLIANCES

When domestic electrical appliances function incorrectly, the first thing to do is to check whether the machine is switched on, and then whether the fuse in the plug, the plug itself and the socket are functioning properly (see **Electrical problems** section). If you've established that they are, see below.

Dishwasher *Unclean crockery and cutlery* You are not using enough detergent, or you need a heavier-duty programme. Make sure that the filter is cleaned regularly.

Spots and streaks on clean crockery You need to soften the water by adding extra salt.

White marks (etching) on glasses Cannot be removed, so valuable glasses should be washed by hand. Etching usually occurs because there is not enough detergent, rinse aid and salt being used.

Damaged cutlery Usually occurs when different metals, such as silver and stainless steel, are washed at the same time. Don't mix them in the cutlery drawer either.

Too much foam You are using the wrong type of detergent. Change brands.

Leaking water The gasket may be dirty, or need replacing.

Electric cooker

If it is just the oven that won't come on, check that it is not switched to automatic.

If food is overcooked or undercooked, make sure that you are not overstacking the oven so that hot air cannot circulate. Learn to live with it and adjust cooking time/temperatures accordingly. If this is too much of a nuisance, get an engineer to correct the thermostat or check temperatures with an oven thermometer.

Microwave cooker

If the cooker doesn't work, the magnetron or other part may have failed and you will need to call the service engineer.

Vacuum cleaner

Check that the fan is working.

Poor suction can mean that the dustbag is full, the filter needs cleaning, the hose isn't attached correctly or has a hole in it or that the roller or belt are worn out and need replacing.

A smell of burning indicates either the need for a new drive belt or that the cleaner has picked up a length of thread or string which has wound itself around the driveshaft.

Replacing a drive belt

- Take details of the name and model number of the cleaner before you buy a new belt.
- Remove the cover either at the front or underneath the cleaner.
- Lift out the roller and remove the damaged belt.
- Slide a new belt over the roller and fit it back into the cleaner.
- Stretch the belt over the drive pulley.
- Replace the cover and check that the cleaner works.

Washing-machine   Check that the water supply is on and that the hoses are not kinked.

If the machine will not spin it may be overloaded. Re-distribute the load, removing some items if necessary. Check that the machine is on the correct programme for spinning.

Too much foam means you are using the wrong detergent. Change it.

FIREPLACES

In general, use a vacuum cleaner attachment to keep a fireplace free from dust and soot.

Brick   Scrub a brick fireplace with a hard brush and clean warm water. Burn marks may respond to sponging with vinegar, then rinsing. Bad soot marks on brick (but not on the cement between the bricks) should be treated with one part spirit of salts (a chemical available from chemists) to six parts water. Wear gloves and protect your eyes.

Cast iron   Remove rust from a cast-iron fireplace with a stiff brush or steel wool (wear goggles). Use a proprietary rust remover to get off the last traces, then apply a thin layer of oil, well rubbed in.

Ceramic tile   These fireplaces just need washing with a household cleaner and an occasional application of an all-purpose polish.

Marble   A marble fireplace should be sponged with a solution of soapflakes, and then rinsed and dried. Apply a special marble polish. There are also products for improving the appearance of worn marble and repairing small chips.

Clean with a solution of washing-up liquid. Rinse *Slate*
and dry. Use marble polish on multi-coloured slate,
nothing on riven slate.

Clean with clear water, using an old clean *Stone*
toothbrush to remove stubborn soot.

FLOORINGS

Keep them swept and, where necessary, washed. Put mats inside all
exit doors and encourage people to remove outdoor shoes when they
come in.

Clean with a solution of washing-up liquid applied *Brick*
with a stiff brush. Rinse and mop dry. Avoid
wetting any more than necessary as bricks are
porous unless treated.

Wash with warm water with a dissolved teacup of *Cement and*
washing soda added. Allow to dry thoroughly. (The *concrete*
floors are easier to clean if they have been sealed.)

Mop with a solution of washing-up liquid, rinse and *Ceramic tiles*
buff with a duster tied around a dry mop head.
Never polish, or the floor will become slippery.
Clean the grouting between the tiles with an old
clean toothbrush.

Sealed cork floors just need mopping over with *Cork*
warm water and the occasional application of a
suitable polish.
Waxed cork floors should be polished with a
non-slip suitable product.

Mop with a solution of general household cleaner, *Linoleum*
but take care not to saturate the floor. When dry,
apply liquid or wax paste polish.

Quarry tiles   Mop with a solution of household cleaner. (You may need to scrub unglazed tiles.) Rinse and mop dry. Use a liquid or wax paste polish on unglazed tiles; nothing on glazed ones.

Where colour has faded, remove traces of polish using fine-grade steel wool and white spirit. Wash and dry, then apply fresh pigmented wax polish. Buff well or the colour will be walked into the rest of the home.

Newly laid quarry tiles may develop white patches as a result of lime in the sub-floor working its way to the top. The patches will fade eventually and can be helped on their way by washing with a solution of 60ml vinegar to five litres of warm water. Do not polish until the marks have disappeared.

Rubber   Wash with a solution of soapflakes, then rinse, dry and apply a suitable emulsion polish.

Stone   Clean with a detergent solution. Stone floors are easier to clean if sealed.

Vinyl   Mop with a solution of household cleaner and apply emulsion polish.

If polish builds up and becomes sticky, remove it either with a manufacturer's recommended polish or a proprietary floor polish remover.

Wood or wood strip   Sweep or vacuum regularly to prevent grit becoming embedded in the wood.

Remove marks with a damp cloth but never wash a whole floor as the wood may swell and warp.

Polish with a proprietary brand polish (an electric polishing machine is useful for large areas).

Where polish has built up, remove it with white spirit applied on a cloth.

Sealed wood floors just need mopping with warm water and an occasional application of a suitable polish.

FURNITURE

You need to clean furniture surfaces regularly; it is not necessary to polish them very often. Once or twice a year is usually enough to maintain a shine and some finishes don't even require that.

Antique

Keep away from radiators and other heat sources or the piece of furniture will dry out and crack. If your home is hot, install a humidifier.
Remove greasy marks and fingerprints with a solution of one part vinegar to eight parts water, applied with a chamois leather and wiped dry immediately. Polish afterwards.

Bamboo

Remove dust with a vacuum cleaner attachment. Once a year take the piece of furniture outside and scrub with a soap solution. Rinse with salted water to keep the bamboo stiff.

French polished

Keep free from dust and polish occasionally with an appropriate product.
Remove marks with white spirit.
Treat scratches with an application of French polish. If a piece is valuable or the scratch is deep, you *must* have it treated professionally.

Leather

Dust frequently and treat occasionally with hide food to maintain sheen and prevent cracking. Make sure that it is rubbed in thoroughly to avoid it coming off on clothes.
Clean the furniture by wiping with a damp cloth wrung out in a soapflake solution. Do not overwet and do not rinse off as the soap helps to keep the leather flexible.
Polish with a soft cloth.
If the leather is specifically non-washable, call in a professional cleaning company.

Lloyd Loom   Blow dust from the crevices using a vacuum cleaner attachment in reverse or use the coolest setting on a hair-dryer.
Clean with a soft nailbrush dipped in a solution of washing-up liquid, then rinse and allow to dry without extra heat.

Painted   Check the finish to make sure that any cleaning other than dusting will not harm it. Check on an unseen patch. If it can be cleaned, use a solution of washing-up liquid.

Upholstered   Dust regularly, for best effect with the soft brush attachment of a vacuum cleaner. Use the crevice tool attachment to get down the back and sides of the upholstery.
Treat spots according to the upholstery fabric (see **Marks and spills** section).
Loose covers can be removed and dry-cleaned or washed according to what they are made of. After washing loose covers, put them back on the furniture while still slightly damp and stretch them into position for a perfect fit. If necessary, iron while in position but don't use too hot a temperature which could damage the padding.
When covers cannot be removed, either use a professional cleaning company or shampoo them yourself, following the manufacturer's instructions.

STICKING DRAWERS

Rub the runners and sides with a piece of soap or a candle. If this doesn't work, wrap a piece of glasspaper around a block or piece of wood and smooth over the runners. Then apply soap or candle wax. Replace damaged runners.

Wood

Oiled wood Should be dusted and re-oiled a couple of times a year.

Sealed wood Just needs dusting. A spray polish will restore shine.

Waxed wood Needs frequent dusting. Apply wax polish if it looks dull but use the minimum quantity, well buffed in. Finger-marks on waxed wood can be removed with a solution of one part vinegar to eight parts warm water. Dry well immediately.

STIFF OR CREAKY HINGES

Drip a few drops of oil into the central spindle of the hinge if you can get at it. Take care that the oil does not drip out and damage the surface of the item. Open and close the door several times to get the hinge working properly again.

If you cannot reach the hinge, spray carefully with an aerosol lubricant, protecting the piece of furniture with kitchen paper or rags.

GAS COOKERS

If your gas cooker functions incorrectly, consider the following points.

- Check that the gas supply is on and any pilot lights lit. Clean the ignition device (instructions for this will be in the manual). If there is still a problem, call the gas engineer.
- If the flames burn unevenly, clean the holes in the burner with a darning needle.

GLASS

**Carafes/
decanters** Remove deposits that won't wash off by filling the carafe with a solution of biological detergent or 30ml salt dissolved in 250ml vinegar. Rinse it in warm water and stand it upside down in a jug or vase to drain.

Chandeliers
- Turn off the electricity at the mains.
- Ideally, remove the pieces separately, clean in a solution of washing-up liquid, rinse and then drain on kitchen paper. Buff with chamois leather. Don't let pieces scratch each other, and make sure you know how to reassemble the chandelier; if necessary, make a diagram as you take it apart.
- Where you can't take it to pieces, stand on a secure pair of steps and rub each chandelier piece with a chamois leather or chamois leather gloves.
- Otherwise, buy a chandelier cleaning spray. Protect the floor below with plastic sheeting or newspaper and spray the glass pieces.

Cookware Wash by hand or use a dishwasher. Remove stuck-on food by soaking.

**Drinking
glasses** Wash in warm water, rinse and dry, or use a dishwasher. Do not wash valuable or delicate glasses in a dishwasher as it can produce 'etching'.

Mirrors Treat with window cleaner. Remove cosmetics from mirrors with methylated spirit.

**Windows and
conservatories**
- Use a proprietary cleaner or a bucket of warm water containing 30ml vinegar. Buff with a chamois leather or crumpled wads of newspaper.
- Pick a dull day to clean windows as sunlight dries the surfaces too quickly and leaves streaks.
- Clean one side of the glass with horizontal strokes, the other with vertical. Then you can see on which side streaks remain.

JEWELLERY

Have valuable jewellery, even if 'fake', cleaned professionally every year or so. It is a good idea to combine the cleaning with revaluation for insurance purposes, especially if it means getting the jewellery out of a bank or safe.

> Never clean jewellery (which can be washed) in a sink; always use a plastic bowl. Use a soft or baby's toothbrush for cleaning intricate pieces and clasps.

Gold chains

Wash in soapy water, rinse and drain on kitchen paper. Rub with a chamois leather.

Hard stones

Hard stones such as amethysts, diamonds, rubies and sapphires should be cleaned in a solution of washing-up liquid, rinsed, then dipped briefly into surgical spirit to remove any film. Drain on kitchen paper and polish with a chamois leather. Alternatively, use a special jewel-cleaning kit, following instructions. Don't let diamonds come into contact with other stones as they will scratch them.

Pearls

These should be worn frequently since the oil from human skin helps to maintain their lustre. Never wash them but rub occasionally with chamois leather. Try not to get perfume, hair spray or foundation make-up directly on them.

Porous stones

Clean porous stones, such as opals, by rubbing them with chamois leather. Do not wet them.

Soft stones

Soft stones, such as emeralds, can be cleaned in the same way as hard stones but should be done separately to ensure they are not knocked together.

KITCHEN EQUIPMENT

Bakeware The less you wash bakeware the better it performs. Ideally, just wipe it with kitchen paper after use.

Very dirty bakeware (though not aluminium or anything with a non-stick coating) should be immersed in a boiling solution of washing soda. Use a preserving pan for this.

Non-stick bakeware is easily cleaned, although some brands recommend that no detergent is used.

Kettles Clean the exterior according to the material it is made from (see **Metals** section and **Plastics** section).

De-fur the interior as soon as signs of scale start to form. Use the product recommended by the manufacturer or a proprietary descaler suitable for the kettle material.

One product, akin to a clump of wire, can be left in a kettle to collect scale.

Knives Check whether they are dishwasher-proof or, if not, wash by hand and dry immediately after use.

Stainless steel blades need no attention; carbon steel blades tend to rust if left damp and wet. Remove dust and food stains with an abrasive cleaning powder. Apply a thin layer of cooking oil to protect the blades. Also oil wooden knife handles from time to time to help prevent splitting.

If you store knives in a drawer they are likely to rub against other implements and become blunt. They are also likely to cut your hands when you rummage in the drawer. Store them in a knife roll, plastic blade covers, in a knife-holding stand or held by their blades on a magnetic wall-mounted rack.

Sinks To clear a blocked sink see **Plumbing** section.

Clean sinks according to manufacturer's instructions and make sure that at the end of each day there are no stains on them.

Do not wash unless really dirty. Use kitchen paper to wipe out salad bowls, and sponge clean cheeseboards and breadboards after use.

Wooden chopping and pastry boards, spoons and rolling pins should be washed up immediately after use and dried.

Wooden items

METALS

When cleaning metals it is important not to scratch them. Always use the correct polish – some metals can take more abrasive ones than others – and make sure it is applied with a soft cloth.

Cooking pans Should be washed and dried immediately after use. Use a steel-wool soap pad to burnish the outside, rinsing thoroughly afterwards.

If food, particularly acid food, is left in an aluminium pan for any length of time, the interior will discolour. Get rid of this by boiling a pan of water containing something acid, such as apple peel, lemon peel or a stick of rhubarb. Rinse immediately and dry.

Anodised aluminium items Items such as trays and trolleys should be cleaned with a damp cloth and dried immediately. Give them a shine with a sparing application of liquid wax polish.

Aluminium

Needs regular cleaning to prevent tarnish. Use a proprietary polish. Very dirty brass can be cleaned with a paste made up of coarse salt and lemon juice. Use an old clean toothbrush to get into any crevices. Rinse immediately and wipe dry.

Lacquered brass Needs wiping over with a damp cloth unless the lacquer has become damaged and tarnish is developing beneath it. In this case, remove all the lacquer with cellulose thinner or nail varnish remover, clean as for bare brass and re-lacquer.

Brass

Bronze Dust regularly. If very dirty, wash in warm soapy water. Apply a little oil occasionally to maintain shine. Cutlery should be hand-washed and dried as soon as possible after use.

Cast iron *Cookware* Wash and dry immediately to prevent rust from developing.

Copper Clean as bronze and polish as necessary.
Cooking pans Clean the outside with a proprietary product or vinegar to which you have added a little salt. The inside of copper pans should always be lined with tin or nickel to prevent an adverse reaction between the copper and certain foods which could cause food poisoning. When the lining starts to wear it should be renewed.

Gold Use a proprietary product to clean, and buff up with a chamois leather.
Gold leaf On picture frames, for example, should be dusted. If it discolours, wipe gently with a solution of 15ml ammonia to 150ml warm water and rinse.

Lead Either leave garden ornaments to weather (no harm will be done) or clean with turpentine and rinse.

Pewter It's not meant to shine like silver but it must be cleaned regularly to prevent build-up of oxide scale. Wash in soapy water; dry thoroughly. Remove finger-marks with methylated spirit and rinse.

Silver Clean and polish regularly with a proprietary product to prevent the build-up of tarnish. Long-term polishes allow you to do this less often but may not clean as well as standard ones.
Silver that is not in regular use should be stored in tarnish-proof bags or wrapped in acid-free tissue paper and kept in an airtight container. Even so, get it out from time to time and clean it.

Stainless steel Wash and dry immediately after use to prevent pitting. Polish occasionally.

MISCELLANEOUS

Wipe with a soft damp cloth. Never wet or immerse as alabaster is porous. **Alabaster**

Dust at least once a year. Remove from the shelf and blow dust off the top of the book to prevent it from dropping between the pages. Use a feather duster to clean the binding.
Leather bindings should be wiped with a damp cloth. Dampen the cloth in a solution of soapflakes to which a little glycerine has been added. **Books**

Decorative Should be protected with a thin film of oil or Vaseline. If rust has developed, remove it with a stiff brush or steel wool (wear goggles to prevent any getting in your eyes). You may need to use a proprietary rust remover if there is a lot. **Cast iron**

Dust but never wash or use a damp cloth. Occasionally, use a little wood furniture cream. **Ebony**

Requires special care when cleaning. Consult a dry cleaner or the textile department of a local museum. **Embroidery**

Stove-enamel Wash in a detergent solution and then spray with an all-purpose polish.
Vitreous enamel Wash in a detergent solution. Clean stubborn marks with a product approved by the Vitreous Enamel Development Council (see **Addresses**). **Enamel**

Clean by moving them around in a soapflake solution, taking care not to wet the back of the brush. Rinse the bristles, then swish in cold water to firm them. Dry naturally with the bristles placed downwards on a towel. **Hairbrush bristles**

Dust with a soft cloth and wipe gently with warm water. Dry immediately. Polish with metal polish (unless they're horn drinking beakers). **Horn**

63

Ivory Dust regularly using a baby's toothbrush for carved areas. Apply a thin layer of almond oil. Because ivory is semi-porous it absorbs liquids such as hairspray (found on the back of hairbrushes, for example).
Knife handles Should not be washed. Only immerse the blades whilst washing-up. Dry immediately.
Piano keys Clean on a regular basis with a warm water and vinegar solution (5ml white vinegar to 250ml water). If discoloured, use a solution of equal parts methylated spirit and warm water. Bad discoloration will require professional scraping; mild discoloration may disappear if you leave the lid open so the sun can bleach the keys. Take care never to get liquid between the keys. Wipe and dry keys immediately after any treatment.

Jade Simply dust. Remove finger-marks with a cloth wrung out in a soapflake solution, then rinse and dry.

Jet Simply dust.

Lacquer Simply dust lacquered metal items.

Mother-of-pearl Take professional advice on cleaning valuable pieces. Avoid washing cutlery handles; clean only the metal parts. Use white cream furniture polish on ornaments. Where the mother-of-pearl is inlaid, apply the polish by finger (wrapped in a soft cloth).

Onyx Onyx is very absorbent, so handle it as little as possible and wipe off spills immediately. Dust to clean. Remove marks with a little methylated spirit.

Papier mâché Simply dust and apply a very fine layer of furniture cream.

Perspex Clean with a solution of washing-up liquid, then rinse and dry. Use a spray polish to prevent it attracting dust. Gently rub on cream metal polish to remove scratches.

Dust with a long-handled feather duster. Use a little furniture cream on wooden frames; touch up gilt frames with a special product available from art shops. *Picture frames*

These collect dust and grease which impair vision. Wash in warm soapy water – ideally daily – and dry gently with a soft, grit-free cloth. Polish with an impregnated cloth (available from opticians) or clean soft cloth and store in a spectacle case when you're not wearing them. *Spectacles*

Wipe with a damp cloth but do not immerse in water. Dry immediately. Buff with a little jeweller's rouge applied on a soft, grit-free cloth. *Tortoiseshell*

PAINTWORK

- Dust using a duster tied over a mop head to reach the tops of walls. *Walls*
- Use a solution of washing-up liquid and wash from the bottom to the top of the wall, not the other way round. This allows any dirty streaks that drip to be wiped off easily. Dirt that drips on to dirt is harder to remove.
- When washing, work over a small area at a time and rinse it before moving to the next.
- Never stop washing in the middle of a wall or a line will appear which will be difficult to remove.
- Very dirty walls should be washed with a solution of sugar soap or household cleaner.

Clean with a general cleaner or a solution of washing-up liquid. Remove grease marks with a non-abrasive household cleaner. *Wood*

PLASTICS

Acrylic   *Baths*   See page 42.
Furniture   Needs wiping with a solution of washing-up liquid. Then rinse and dry. Remove scratches by rubbing gently with cream metal polish.
Kitchen utensils   Wash by hand or in a dishwasher.

Laminated   Use a non-abrasive household cleaner or the
surfaces   product recommended by the manufacturer.

Melamine   Follow manufacturer's recommendations. Remove stains by soaking the item in a very mild solution of household bleach.

Vinyl   See page 54.

SAUCEPANS/COOKWARE

Burnt pans   Soak overnight with a solution of biological detergent made up according to the manufacturer's instructions. Bring the solution to the boil and then tip away. Carefully scrape off the loosened deposit and clean the pan as usual.

Non-stick pan   Follow manufacturer's instructions and treat with
linings   care, even if the surface claims to withstand metal implements. To remove any build-up, rub gently with a wet nylon cleaning pad.
To remove staining, boil a solution of 250ml water, 50ml household bleach and 30ml bicarbonate of soda for five minutes. Clean the pan as usual and apply a thin layer of cooking oil to re-season it.

Getting rid of smells

• In the kitchen   • Elsewhere

There are many ways in which smells can build up; opening windows and doors will help to dispel them, as will the use of electric fan devices containing filters. Below are some specific remedies for the most common household smells.

IN THE KITCHEN

Use bin-liners in your kitchen bins – you can buy scented ones which help if your bin doesn't get filled up quickly. Wash or soak bins regularly in a solution of household bleach.

Bins

Foodstuffs like fish, garlic and onions tend to leave smells on wooden chopping boards. Rub boards with a lemon before washing to dispel the smells. Plastic boards harbour smells less and can be cleaned thoroughly in a dishwasher.

Chopping board

Where appropriate, cover food tightly while cooking. Use a layer of foil if the pan and lid don't fit well together. Install a cooker hood, which will either vent smells to outside the home via a duct or re-circulate smelly air through a charcoal filter.

Cooking

> Don't let smells linger, otherwise they will become impossible to dispel.

Dishwasher   Clean the filter at least once a week and whenever it looks clogged. If you don't use the machine every day, run a rinse cycle over dirty dishes stacked in it. From time to time, run the machine whilst it is empty with a special dishwasher cleaning product. You can buy lemon-scented sachets to hang from the top rack which keep it smelling pleasant for several cycles (see also **Dishwashers** in **Household and cleaning problems** section).

Drains   Check for grease or debris and clean thoroughly using caustic soda and hot water. Protect your hands and be careful not to get splashes on your clothes. Clear any blockage which may be causing the smell (see also **Plumbing problems** section).

Hands   Don't wash your hands immediately in hot water as it tends to 'set' the smell. Rub with a cut lemon, some vinegar or salt and rinse well in tepid water. Repeat until the smell disappears.

Microwave   Place a bowl of water containing some lemon juice in the oven and cook on high for five minutes. Wipe out the resulting condensation with a clean cloth.

Plastic boxes   Fill plastic storage boxes with a solution of bicarbonate of soda (15ml to 500ml of warm water) and leave overnight before rinsing well.

Refrigerator   Clean your fridge out frequently. Washing with a solution of bicarbonate of soda (15ml to 500ml of warm water) is usually better than using a brand-name cleaner which may leave its own smell. Cover food in the fridge and place a charcoal-filled device, such as a 'fridge egg', inside to absorb odours, particularly if you are going away and want to switch off the fridge and leave the door closed.

Boil a pan of water containing 45ml vinegar, then leave it to cool. Rinse well afterwards. *Saucepans*

To freshen up your waste-disposal unit, grind up some orange or lemon peel. *Waste-disposal units*

ELSEWHERE

Use an electric air filter or fan to refresh the air. A dish of vinegar in the room will help, as will lighting a candle, especially one designed to remove smoke smells. *Cigarettes*

Wash or dry-clean clothes frequently and always allow them to air before putting away after wearing. If you perspire a lot, stitch armpit shields into your clothes and wash or dispose of the shields as necessary. *Clothes*

Slice an onion in half and leave it cut side up near the recently painted surface overnight. Throw away the onion afterwards. *Paint*

Groom pets regularly and wash bedding frequently. If pet mess produces smelly carpets, use a brand-name cleaning product or sprinkle with baking powder, then leave for an hour before vacuuming (see also **Urine** and **Vomit** in **Marks and spills**). Consult a vet if a pet is persistently smelly for no apparent reason. *Pets*

For instant treatment, strike a match or light a candle. Keep the toilet clean and well ventilated, if possible. Otherwise, keep a scented air-freshener handy. *Toilets*

69

Problems with pests

● Insects   ● Other pests

O ne person's pet can be another's pest. Here's how to deal with the most common species of livestock that no one wants in and around the home.

INSECTS

Ants A kettleful of boiling water will kill any ants you see marching around but won't destroy the nest. Buy an ant killer in spray, powder or jelly form and follow the instructions carefully, taking note of any dangers to pets or wildlife. Treat skirting-boards and doorways with an insecticidal lacquer.

Bed bugs Bed bugs are round, mahogany-coloured creatures about 6mm long. They like living in bedrooms and biting at night. Call in the local pest control department.

Bees/swarms Stay clear of them and call in a local beekeeper. There should be a list of beekeepers with the local authority pest control department, in the public library and with the police.

Bluebottles Attack bluebottles with a fly spray and keep an insecticidal strip or electric zapper in your kitchen. Always keep food and food waste covered, and from time to time treat your dustbin with an insecticidal powder.

Get rid of the fluff that attracts carpet beetles. **Carpet beetles**
Vacuum carpets and use vacuum cleaner tools to
clean out wardrobes and cupboards (especially the
airing cupboard). Spray carpet beetle killer into the
cracks between floorboards. Dry-clean or wash
clothes and blankets that have been infested.

Keep unused blankets, sweaters and so on in sealed **Clothes moths**
plastic bags. Spray carpets and curtains with
moth-proofer. Use a moth repellent in wardrobes
and cupboards where fabrics are stored.

Cockroaches are around 1 to 4½cm long and are **Cockroaches**
remarkably difficult to kill with insecticide, although
it's worth trying if there are only a few. For dealing
with a serious infestation, call in the local
authority's pest control department.

Treat a manageable outbreak with repeated **Death-watch**
applications of a brand-name woodworm killer. To **beetles**
solve a serious problem, call in a wood preservation
company.

Fleas tend to be brought in by cats and dogs, so **Fleas**
spray pets with a flea killer supplied by a vet.
Vacuum carpets thoroughly and spray them with
flea killer. Wash pets' bedding regularly and treat
with flea powder.

Treat in the same way as bluebottles. **Flies (house)**

Flour beetles (weevils) live on stored dry foods such **Flour beetles**
as flour and cereals. Throw infested food away – or,
if you think you bought infested food, complain to
the shop in question and, if necessary, to the local
authority's environmental health department.
Clean out food cupboards thoroughly and make
sure they are completely dry before replacing food
in them. Treat surfaces with an insecticide designed
for stored food products. Keep all dry foods in
sealed containers.

Lice Head lice are usually brought home by schoolchildren and produce an itching scalp. All members of the household should be treated with special shampoo, even if only one person actually appears to have lice. Schools usually notify parents if there is an outbreak of lice and recommend an appropriate product. Otherwise, consult a pharmacist or GP.

Mosquitoes Clean out damp areas, such as water butts and bird baths, as they are potential breeding grounds. Fix flyscreens over open doors and windows. Apply mosquito repellent to exposed areas of your skin and burn mosquito coils (taking care not to create a fire risk).

Silverfish Silverfish are silver-coloured, carrot-shaped creatures around 12mm long. They like the damp areas of kitchens and bathrooms, so try to eliminate these. Treat silverfish with an insecticide designed for crawling insects.

Wasps Keep wasps out of the home by fitting screens or keeping windows closed. Spray with a wasp killer or trap them in jars filled with water with a sweet sticky substance, such as jam, smeared around the top. Cover with paper in which you have made a couple of holes large enough for the wasp to get in through. Getting out again is virtually impossible and they drown when exhausted. If you have a wasps' nest, call in your local authority's pest control department.

Woodworm Woodworm are actually bettles rather than worms and should be treated by applying woodworm killer with an applicator to get the fluid into holes. Large areas of woodworm require the attention of a specialist pest control firm.

OTHER PESTS

Bats are a totally protected species under the **Bats**
Wildlife and Countryside Act 1981. If you find any
kind of bat in your home, get in touch with English
Nature (0733 340345) who will advise you on what
to do.

Birds are usually harmless unless they irritate you as **Birds**
they walk about on a flat roof. Since this is done
mainly by pigeons, which are classified as vermin,
you may put down poison. This can be supplied by
a vet. You must take great care not to kill any local
cats or dogs. Birds which poke milk-bottle tops can
be foiled if you ask the milkman to upend old (clean)
tin cans, mugs or any other receptacle that's heavy
enough to withstand wind blowing over the top.

In rural areas, foxes can be hunted or shot. In town, **Foxes**
where they feed on household rubbish, it is virtually
impossible to do anything about them other than
keeping your rubbish in solid, closed bins.

Put down baited traps (humane ones which don't **Mice**
kill the mouse are available). Block up visible mouse
entry holes with wire wool held in place with
cement filler. If the problem persists, get a cat or call
in your local authority's pest control department.

Buy rat poison or consult your local authority's pest **Rats**
control department.

Put down slug pellets (available from garden **Slugs**
centres). These may be harmful to dogs and cats, so
conceal them under tiles, slates or leaves.
Alternatively, surround precious plants with
something sharp – coarse sand, gorse clippings or
bonfire ashes – which will repel the slugs.

73

Squirrels   Squirrels can be shot but not, by law, poisoned unless you have special dispensation for this. If they are in your roof, try to chase them out and then block up the holes by which they came in. If squirrels are persistent, call in the environmental health department or a specialist pest control firm to set traps.

A useful book, *The A-Z of Household Pests*, is available from the British Pest Control Association (see **Addresses**) for £2.50 inc. p&p.

Sewing and mending tips

● Buttons ● Holes
● Miscellaneous ● Zips

I f you know how to mend fabrics you can get extra wear from them.
Otherwise, find the cheat's way of solving sewing problems.

BUTTONS

● When replacing a button, don't sew it tightly on to the fabric: it
  needs a shank to allow the outer layer of material to fit over it.
● As you draw the first thread up and down through the holes in the
  button, leave about 50mm (¼in) between the button and the
  garment – more, ideally, with thick fabric. Hold the button away
  from the fabric as you stitch.
● When you have created a shank of several threads (using all the
  holes on the button), wind the thread around the shank several
  times before finishing off firmly with several small stitches on the
  back of the fabric.

As an emergency measure, always carry a
safety pin around with you, either in a
handbag or pinned to the inside of a pocket.

HOLES

In fabrics Holes in fabric which cannot be darned need to be patched. Use a matching piece of fabric – either an offcut or a piece snipped from inside a hem.

- Cut the piece about 5cm (2in) larger than the hole, if possible, making sure that the pattern matches.
- Trim the hole to a square or rectangular shape and cut a 5mm (¼in) diagonal at each corner.
- Turn the garment inside out (turn table linen, etc. upside down) and place the patch over the underside of the hole, right side to the wrong side of the fabric.
- Pin and tack into position.
- Turn the item right way out and turn under the edges of the hole.
- Slip stitch the patch into position, remove tacking and press.

In pockets
- Turn the garment inside out and cut out the old pocket, leaving 5cm (2in) of fabric in place. (Cut in a straight line.)
- Turn the cut-out pocket inside out, pin it to a piece of paper and draw around it, allowing a 2.5cm (1in) allowance all round. Then you need to use the paper template to cut out a shape from the material. Check that the grain of the fabric runs the same way as that of the original fabric.
- Stitch a French seam round the curved edge but leave the straight side open. Press.
- Turn the new pocket right side out.
- Pull the remaining fabric from the old pocket through to the right side of the trousers.
- Pin the pocket to it, allowing 2.5cm (1in) overlap.
- Turn the visible edge of the new pocket under, tack, then stitch into position. Remove tacking.
- Pull the pocket into position inside the garment and turn the remaining raw edge under. Stitch neatly and press.

FRENCH SEAM

Place pieces wrong sides together and sew along the length 1cm from the edge. Trim the seam allowance. Turn the fabrics right sides together and sew a second line 1cm from the new edge to create a tube with the first seam inside it.

Darning is always easier to do before a garment has a hole worn through it.

In woollens

- Use a darning needle of a suitable size and matching thread or wool. The process is also easier if you use a darning mushroom (from haberdashery departments).
- Make a frame of running stitches round the hole, about 2.5cm (1in) from the edges. This strengthens the area.
- Darning is really weaving. Stitch a warp of threads across the hole in one direction. Make sure it is not too tight to allow for the thread shrinking (the rest of the garment will have shrunk during previous washings/cleanings) and to accommodate bending elbows, for example.
- Next, weave the thread through the rows with an over-and-under stitch that alternates on each row.
- For large holes and repairs to table linen, tack a patch of net or muslin to the underside of the hole and work the stitches through this for a firmer result.

You can shrink thread or wool to be used for darning. Steam it over a pan of boiling water or hold it (using an oven glove) in the steam from a kettle. Dry before use.

MISCELLANEOUS

Duvet refilling
- Shake the existing filling to one end of the duvet and tie a piece of string around the area which contains it.
- Either unpick the other end (with a stitch ripper) or cut it open, taking off as little fabric as possible.
- Take handfuls of the appropriate matching filling and push it into the channels.
- When full, pin and tack tightly across the open end, remove the string and shake the duvet to check whether there is too much or too little filling.
- Remove temporary tacking and fold the raw edges of the duvet under. Pin and tack.
- Machine a double line of stitching across the opening.

Elastic
Broken Replace broken elastic by stitching new elastic firmly into a bodkin or safety pin and easing it through the pocket of material, e.g. a waistband.
Worn With worn elastic, stitch one end of the new elastic to the old and pull the old out and the new length through.

Dropped hems
- Unless only a few stitches have gone and the hem can be repaired easily, take down the whole hem. Brush off any debris that has collected inside it.
- Pin up at 2.5cm (1in) intervals, making sure that the original hemline stays in position. Pleat as necessary. Tack into position, remove pins and press.
- Slip stitch neatly into position and remove tacking.

> In a hurry, use an iron-on bonding tape. This works for curtains and blinds as well.

Stop the run with nail varnish (clear, if possible) or soap that has been lightly moistened.

Laddered tights

Use a sewing-machine or neat back stitch to repair. Make sure that the line of stitching extends at least 2.5cm (1in) beyond the split at both ends.

Split seams

Tears

- Place the edges of the tear together and tack a piece of stiff paper behind them. Alternatively, iron on a piece of bonding web.
- Using matching thread, stitch the edges of the tear together using small neat slanting stitches and going through the paper or bonding web.
- Finish off securely and tear away the paper on either side of the mend.
- Alternatively, apply an iron-on patch or use iron-on bonding web to mend the tear without stitching. Cut a piece of matching fabric (pattern also matching where possible) from the inside of a hem or seam. Use a large enough piece of bonding web to fix the two pieces of fabric together.

ZIPS

Seam opening

New zip insertion

- First tack together the seam of the garment as if there were no zip. Press.
- Pin and tack the zip into position. Remove pins.
- Machine-stitch around the edges and remove tacking. Press.

Slit opening

- Mark the stitch lines with a line of tacking down both sides and across the base.
- Place the zip under the opening with its slider closed. Check it is even all the way down. Pin and tack into position.

- Remove pins and check that the zip runs freely.
- Machine-stitch into position 3mm from the edge of the metal.
- Remove tacking and press.

In an emergency, get hold of a needle and thread and stitch yourself into the garment. Replace the zip when you get home.

Removing a broken zip

- Remove the broken zip using a stitch ripper. Take out all loose threads and press turnings.
- Ideally, use a zipper foot on a sewing-machine to put in the new zip and follow the former stitch lines. Without one, use a neat back stitch.

New zip slider

Where a zip slider on a bag has become worn and doesn't fasten the teeth together, it can be replaced without having to replace the entire zip.

- With a screwdriver, lever off the zip stop at the bottom of the existing zip.
- Pull the slider down and off the zip.
- Slip on a new slider (the best way is to cannibalise an old zip) and half close the zip.
- Push the prongs of the new stop (also cannibalised from another zip) into the holes left by the old one. Press the prongs flat, using the blade of a small screwdriver.

JAMMED ZIP

Coat the open teeth near the jam with soap or candle wax. Gently ease the slider backwards and forwards until the jam is clear.

2

WIRES AND PIPES

Electrical and gas problems
Plumbing problems
Cutting heating bills

Electrical and gas problems

- Basic tool kit • Wiring a 13-amp plug
- Changing fuses • D-i-y projects
- Power cuts • Gas leaks

Electricity can kill, so don't attempt any electrical work if you are unsure of what to do. Unless you are an expert, major jobs should be left to a professional. But the following common problems can be dealt with without much difficulty.

BASIC TOOL KIT

Keep it handy in case you have to work in darkness if, say, a fuse has blown.
- medium (6mm blade) screwdriver
- small (3mm blade) screwdriver, preferably a tester (incorporates a small light that illuminates when in contact with a live wire)
Both screwdrivers should have plastic handles and insulation running about halfway down the shaft
- pliers with cutting edges and insulated handles
- wire stripping tool
- sharp craft knife
- selection of fuses and fuse wire, including cartridge fuses if you have a mains fuse box which takes this type
- freestanding torch.

WIRING A 13-AMP PLUG

Make sure that any plug you buy is marked 'made to BS 1363' and carries the ASTA mark.
The wires in a flex are colour coded

brown   = live
blue   = neutral
green and yellow   = earth

[The colours in older plugs are red for live, blue for neutral and green for earth.]

The terminals to which each wire should be connected carry the initials

L
N
E or ⏚ symbol

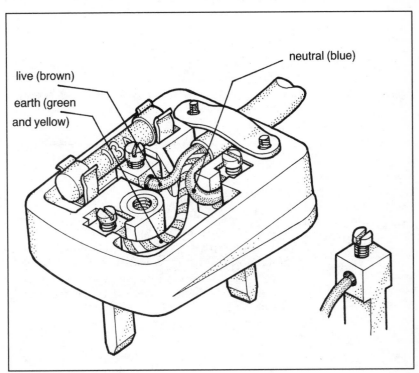

live (brown)

earth (green
and yellow)

neutral (blue)

- Use a screwdriver to undo the centre screw of the plug and remove the top cover. Loosen the two smaller screws that hold the cord-grip in position and remove one. Push the cord-grip to one side.
- Take out the fuse.
- Loosen the screws at the terminals but leave them in place.
- Trim with a knife the outer casing of the flex by about 38mm (1½in), taking care not to cut the inner wires.
- Strip back the coloured insulation from the three wires by about 6mm (¼in).
- Twist together the strands of wire and place into the correct terminals (see diagram); tighten the screws so that the wire is held in place with no loose strands.
- For stud terminals, wind the wire around the stud in a clockwise direction.
- Replace the fuse.
- Replace the screw in the cord-grip and tighten both screws to grip the outer casing of the flex firmly. Give the cord a sharp tug to check.
- Replace the plug top cover and tighten the central screw.

Changing a plug fuse   A plug fuse should be marked 'made to BS 1362' and carry the ASTA mark.

If the plug has a lift-up lid to the fuse carrier, raise it and remove and replace the fuse. Otherwise, merely take off the cover and replace the fuse.

FUSES

Opposite is a list of appliances which require a 3-amp or 13-amp fuse. But because some appliances vary widely in their wattage rating it is important to check the manufacturer's handbook to ensure you fit the correct fuse. Some television manufacturers recommend the use of a 5-amp fuse. Again, check the handbook.

Use a 3-amp (red) fuse for appliances rated up to 720 watts. These include:

clock
coffee-grinder
electric blanket*
extractor fan
food processor/
    blender
hair-dryer*
heated rollers
lamp
radio
sewing-machine
slide projector
slow cooker
tape recorder
TV
waste-disposal unit.

Use a 13-amp (brown) fuse for appliances rated between 720 and 3000 watts. These include:

deep-fat fryer
dishwasher
fan heater
fires*
iron
kettle
refrigerator
spin-dryer
TV (colour)
toaster
tumble-dryer
vacuum cleaner
washing-machine.

* Check the exact wattage.

CHANGING FUSES

If all the lights in one area go out or several appliances stop working at the same time, a fuse in the main fuse box has probably blown. You need to replace it and find out what caused the problem and disconnect it, or the fuse will blow again.

Main fuse

- First, switch off all the lights and appliances on the circuit. Check to see if there is any visible damage (e.g. a loose or chopped wire, scorch marks around a plug). If nothing is apparent, replace the fuse (see below), then switch on lights and appliances one at a time. Somewhere along the line the fuse will blow again and will need replacing, but you will have identified the problem. If a fuse keeps blowing, call an electrician. Make sure you're not overloading the circuit. Add up the wattage of all the lights/appliances on it.

- A lighting circuit should carry no more than 1200 watts.
- A socket outlet should carry no more than 7200 watts.

Cartridge type
- Turn off the mains switch in the fuse box (also called the consumer unit).
- Switch off appliances or lights on the circuit.
- Take out the fuse carrier.
- Replace the faulty circuit cartridge with a new one of the rating which is shown on the fuse carrier.
- Replace the fuse carrier, close unit and switch on mains electricity.
- Check the circuit (see above).

Rewirable type
- Switch off the mains switch in the fuse box (consumer unit).
- Switch off and unplug appliances or lights on the circuit.
- Find out which fuse has blown. If they're not labelled, look for scorch marks and, failing that, check each fuse individually for broken wire by pulling the fuse carrier out of the box.
- Loosen the two screws on the fuse carrier and remove the broken wire.
- Cut new wire of the correct amp rating. It should be long enough to cross the carrier and go round both screws with some slack to allow for tightening them.
- Wind the wire clockwise round one screw and tighten it.
- Take the length to the second screw, using the same route as in another fuse carrier (take one out to check).
- Wind the wire clockwise round the second screw, leaving some slack.

- Tighten the screw.
- Replace the fuse carrier, close the fuse box and switch on the mains electricity.
- Check the circuit (see above).

Cookers and immersion heaters have dedicated fuses in the main fuse box or near to the site. If these have blown, it is advisable to call in an electrician.

Dedicated fuses

If your fuse box (consumer unit) has miniature circuit breakers you can see immediately which current is faulty.

Miniature circuit breakers

- Turn off the mains switch.
- Switch off appliances or lights.
- Reset the circuit breaker.
- Turn on the mains switch.
- Check the circuit (see above).

D-I-Y PROJECTS

An extended flex is useful on items such as lamps, kitchen appliances and sewing-machines, but with power tools and vacuum cleaners it is better to use an extension lead which should be fully unwound or uncoiled during use to prevent it heating up.

Extending a flex

Never extend a flex by joining wires with insulating tape.

Buy the correct flex (two or three strand) and ampage and a special flex connector.
- Remove the plug from the appliance.
- Take off the flex connector cover.
- Trim back the outer casing of the flex to expose the wires.

- Push the flex through the rubber sleeve of the connector and position it in the cord-grip, leaving enough wire to connect to the terminals.
- Trim back the insulation on the wires, if necessary.
- Twist together loose strands and connect the wires to the correct terminals.
- Tighten the cord-grip screws and replace the cover.

It is advisable that the earth wire is run between the neutral and live wires.

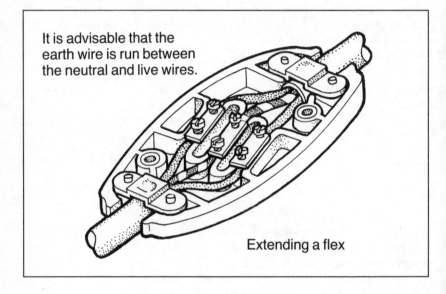

Extending a flex

Fitting a
ceiling
lampholder

- Switch off the electricity at the mains and remove the appropriate fuse from the fuse box.
- Check that the light doesn't come on.
- Remove lampshade bulb and old holder.
- Trim back the insulation on the hanging flex.
- Twist the wires of each thread together and bend back at the end to make threading easier.

Metal fittings on ceiling holders need earthing.

- Unscrew the top of the new holder and thread the flex through it.
- Put the leads into position on each side of the anchorage on the holder.
- Connect a wire to each terminal and tighten the screws.
- Screw the two parts of the holder together.
- Refit the bulb and lampshade.
- Replace the fuse in the fuse box and switch on at the mains.
- Follow this same procedure for other lamps.

Fitting a dimmer switch

- Switch off the electricity at the mains and remove the appropriate fuse from the fuse box.
- Check that the light does not come on.
- Undo screws holding existing light panel against the wall box.
- Pull switch panel towards you and undo the live and neutral wires from the terminals. *Do not* undo the earth wire attached to the wall box.
- Check the instructions supplied with the dimmer switch and reconnect the wires to the correct terminals.
- Position the dimmer switch in the wall box and fix it in place with the screws provided.
- Replace the fuse in the fuse box and switch on the electricity.
- Check that the dimming effect is functioning properly.

Replacing the starter on a fluorescent light fitting

- When a fluorescent tube flickers or fails to light properly it is probably the starter that has failed.
- Switch off the electricity at the mains and remove the fuse from the fuse box.
- You will find the starter either projecting from the side or inside the casing of the fitting. It is canister shaped.
- Unscrew it anticlockwise and take it with you to buy the correct new one.
- Screw in the new starter clockwise.
- Replace the fuse in the fuse box and switch on the electricity. Check whether the light works.

Doubling up a
single socket
outlet

- Switch off the electricity at the mains and remove the appropriate fuse from the fuse box.
- Check that the existing socket is not working by plugging in a lamp or something similar.
- Unscrew the screws that hold the socket into the wall box.
- Pull the socket towards you and carefully unscrew the terminal screws behind.
- Remove the cables from the terminals and take off the existing socket.
- Check that the existing cables are long enough to fit to a double socket outlet. If not, call in a professional.
- Unscrew the wall box and remove it from the wall cavity.
- Place the new box against the wall and mark its outline on the wall.
- With a hammer and chisel, cut away the plaster and brickwork within the outline. Avoid damaging the cables or making a hole that is too big.
- With a masonry bit, drill new fixing holes in the brickwork and fit wall plugs into them.
- Knock out the metal entry discs in the box and pull the cables through.
- Fix the box in position with screws, and plaster around the edges. Leave to dry overnight.
- Connect the cables within the new socket outlet. Red goes to live, black to neutral and green/yellow to earth.
- Replace the fuse

Surface-mounted box The procedure is similar but simpler as the new box can easily be screwed to the skirting-board.

Replacing an
electric fire
element

- Unplug the fire at the socket or, if it is fixed into the supply, switch off the electricity at the mains and remove the appropriate fuse.
- Unclip or unscrew the safety guard.
- Remove the end covers from the element.
- Unscrew the terminal nuts using grips or pliers.
- Remove element from the fire.

- Take the opportunity to clean up the terminals with glasspaper and to clean and buff up the reflector.
- Take the old element with you to check the replacement is the same size and type.
- Fit the new element, reassemble the fire, replace the guard (and fuse if appropriate) and check that the fire works.

Replacing the flex on an iron

- Remove the plug from the iron.
- Remove the terminal cover or back panel of the iron and lift it off.
- Undo the terminal wires, making a small diagram to show where each one goes.
- Take the old flex with you to buy a new one.
- Strip back the outer casing on the new flex by about 5cm (2in) and strip each core wire back about 6mm (¼in).
- Twist together the wires and connect them to the correct terminals. Tighten.
- Replace the iron cover or back panel and fit a plug to the other end of the flex (see **Wiring a plug** above).

Christmas tree lights

- Store carefully between seasons.
- Keep a supply of the correct spare bulbs.
- Test the lights before putting them on the tree.
- If the lights do not work, check that all the bulbs are screwed/pushed in tightly.
- If the lights still do not work, replace the fuse bulb (white tipped) with a new one.

POWER CUTS

- Check whether the power cut is widespread (look at neighbours' windows) or only in your own home.
- If only in your home, test the various circuits to see which fuse(s) has blown and replace (see **Changing fuses**, page 85).

- If a general power cut, switch off all appliances apart from the freezer and refrigerator (and clocks that use very little power). A sudden surge of electricity when power is restored could blow a fuse if several high-consumption appliances, such as fires, are left on. Switch on one light so you'll know when the power returns.
- If you have advance warning of a power cut, get organised. Switch fridge and freezer controls to maximum up to 24 hours ahead and don't open the freezer during the power cut. Make sure you have torches and candles handy, an alternative source of heating (paraffin, camping gas) if necessary, and a method of heating food and drink.
- When the power returns, reset clocks and time switches. Do not open the freezer for a further six hours. See **Freezer emergencies** in the **Food and the kitchen** section for safe storage periods for frozen food.

GAS LEAKS

- If you smell gas, extinguish cigarettes and any naked flames. Switch off machines, such as a vacuum cleaner, which could produce a spark that would ignite the gas. *Don't* switch lights on *or* off.
- Turn off the gas tap next to the meter by setting the handle at right angles to the pipe.
- Open windows.
- Call the gas company's emergency service (if you can't get through, dial 999 and ask for 'Police').
- Leave the building and warn neighbours.
- *Do not* attempt any rescue or repair measures yourself.
- Have gas appliances serviced regularly.

All gas maintenance must, by law, be carried out by a trained engineer authorised by British Gas or the Council for Registered Gas Installers (CORGI) – see **Addresses**.

Plumbing problems

- Prevention   • Basic tool kit
- Water systems   • Baths
- Miscellaneous   • Pipes
- Radiators   • Sinks
- Taps   • Toilets

Serious faults need attention from a professionally qualified plumber but you can fix a lot of small problems yourself. Don't attempt home repairs unless you feel confident you can carry them out successfully.

PREVENTION

You should familiarise yourself with your home's plumbing system *before* anything goes wrong. The most important thing to know is where the main stopcock is sited. As long as you can turn this off, you will be able to prevent serious flooding in the event of a burst pipe. In most homes the stopcock is sited where the water supply comes into the house, usually in a cellar, kitchen (under the kitchen sink) or under the stairs. To check that a stopcock works, turn it off completely (turning clockwise) and turn on the kitchen tap. Water should eventually stop flowing; if it doesn't, the washer on the stopcock is probably not functioning and you will need to get a plumber to replace it. Make a habit of turning the stopcock on and off two or three times a year to prevent it from jamming. If it's very stiff, apply some penetrating oil and check that the weakest-wristed member of your household is able to turn it in an emergency.

BASIC TOOL KIT

- adjustable spanner with jaws opening to 2.5cm (1in)
- set of open-ended spanners
- pliers
- adjustable grips
- blowtorch
- cup plungers for dealing with blockages.

WATER SYSTEMS

Draining   Draining the water systems can be a sensible precaution if you are leaving your home unheated for a long spell in cold weather.

Cold water system   Close the main stopcock, then turn on all the cold taps and flush all the toilets until the water stops flowing. This drains the storage cistern and reduces the water level to its lowest point, which is usually just below the kitchen tap. You can also drain the last pipe but it is not essential.

Hot water system   Switch off the boiler and immersion heater and allow time for the water to cool. Turn on all the hot taps until the system is empty.

Hot water cylinder   Open the draincock where the pipe from the cistern enters it. Use a hose attached to the cock to drain water into a sink or container at a lower level.

Boiler and heating system   Attach a hose to the draincock and run it to a drain below the boiler level. Open the draincock and, when the water flows, open the air vents on the upstairs radiators.

When the system is completely empty, close all the draincocks just in case you forget to do this when you come to refill.

Refilling

- Check that the taps are turned off and that air vents and draincocks are closed.
- Open the main stopcock.
- Turn on all the taps until water is flowing steadily. This is in order to prevent airlocks.

Preventing corrosion

Radiators With an existing system, drain it down, flush it through with clean water and refill with special anti-corrosion liquid of the type recommended by the manufacturer.

- With a new system, where water is already clean, add the liquid to the expansion tank, then draw off enough water from one of the draincocks to allow the liquid to be absorbed into the system. The expansion tank is the one that keeps the central heating system topped up; it is normally found in the loft.

Curing airlocks

An airlock in the system means that water comes out of taps in fits and starts – or not at all. It is usually caused after a lot of water has been drawn off the system and when air has got into the pipes.

- Try letting the taps run until water starts to flow properly.
- If this fails, clip one end of a garden hose to a mains tap (usually the kitchen cold water tap) with a hose connector and the other to the faulty tap. Turn on the faulty tap, then turn on the mains tap. Pressure of water should blow the air out of the pipe. The hose connector on the mains tap should incorporate a double-check valve to guard against any risk of back-siphonage. Turn off the taps when the noise of the air has stopped.
- Disconnect the hose from the mains tap and let it drain before disconnecting the other end.

BATHS

If the area around the bath leaks, you need to replace or fit sealant by one of three methods. First, however, remove all sealant and make sure all surfaces are dry.

Ceramic tile quadrants   Fit ceramic tile quadrants (available in standard tile colours) round the bath. These are suitable for metal baths only.

- Use a tile cutter to get the right lengths at the ends of the runs.
- Use tile adhesive to stick the tiles to the wall and silicone rubber sealant to stick them to the bath edge. Wait for the tiles to dry before using the bath.

Flexible plastic strips   They come with built-in adhesive backing and are pressed into place. They can be cut to the desired length with scissors.

Silicone rubber sealant
- Buy a sealant gun (from d-i-y stores) and a tube of silicone rubber sealant (available in various colours to match the bath).
- Decide on the width of the seal and apply strips of masking tape along the bath and wall, leaving a gap of the size you require. Do not expect silicone to bridge gaps wider than about 6mm (¼ in).
- If you have a plastic bath, remember to fill it with water before starting.
- Apply the sealant following the manufacturer's instructions.
- Run a wet finger along the seal to produce a smooth finish, or angle the nozzle.
- Remove the masking tape while the sealant is still wet.
- Don't touch the sealant or use the bath until the sealant is quite dry.

MISCELLANEOUS

- Unscrew the nozzle from the pipes, using pipe grips round a protective cloth if it is stiff.

  Furred-up shower head

- Put the shower head into a container and pour in a proprietary descaler made up according to the manufacturer's instructions.
- If scale is very bad, you'll need to use a thin skewer or darning needle to poke scale out of the individual holes.
- Rinse thoroughly and reassemble.

- Provided your pipework is standard, this is a simple task but check with your local water company whether any special regulations apply.

  Plumbing-in a washing-machine

- Buy a plumbing-in kit from a d-i-y store. For a washing-machine you will need one to connect to the hot and one to the cold water systems. (Cold-fill-only washing-machines are easier to plumb-in.)
- Follow the instructions supplied with the kit.

If discoloured water comes out of your tap it usually means the water company has been working on the supply pipes. If it doesn't clear after running the tap for a few minutes, contact the water company (address and telephone number are on your bill).

Dirty water

PIPES

You'll need a plumber for a major repair but can effect a temporary one by turning off the boiler, appropriate stopcock(s) and draining the system of water (see above).

Burst pipes

- As a stop-gap measure, apply a bandage and epoxy resin adhesive. Apply adhesive to the pipe, wind the bandage around twice, apply more adhesive, and so on. Wear protective gloves.

Noisy pipes
- Check that all pipes are fixed securely in pipe clips.
- Fit a larger ball float in the main storage cistern.
- Replace the existing ball valve with an equilibrium ball valve which will oscillate less under mains pressure.
- Try closing the main stopcock slightly.

Thawing pipes
Pipes, especially those running through exposed areas such as external walls, should be insulated. Wrap them with overlapping lagging tape or use special split lengths of insulating foam. However, if your pipes do freeze up, follow the instructions below.
- If possible, feel along the length of the pipe to find the frozen section. Otherwise, you'll have to make a guess.
- Either wrap old towels/rags round it and apply a filled hot-water bottle or a kettleful of boiling water to them or play the heat from a hair-dryer or fan heater along the pipe. Don't get too close or the pipes will buckle and melt. Continue gently till the blockage is thawed.
- If the pipe has split and leaks when thawed, turn off the stopvalve on it and then drain the cold water system (see above).
- Make a temporary repair to a damaged pipe by wrapping it with dry joint-sealing tape.

RADIATORS

When air is trapped within the heating system it rises to the top of the radiators and prevents them from fully filling with hot water.

Bleeding radiators

- Open the air vent screw at the end of the radiator using the key provided (or buy a new radiator key from a d-i-y store).
- Have a cup or bowl ready to catch the water. When it flows out steadily, close the air vent.

SINKS

If you must pour away fat or grease (better done in an outside drain), follow this with two or three full kettles of boiling water. With bathroom basins, remove hairs, etc. on a regular basis.

Unblocking sinks

- Bale out as much water as possible.
- Mix a solution of caustic soda and hot water and pour it down the drain. Wear protective goggles and gloves.
- If this fails, stuff a rag into the overflow outlet and buy a special plunger from a hardware store or d-i-y outlet.
- Apply a thin layer of petroleum jelly to the plunger's rim and place the cup over the drain. Run into the sink enough water to cover the cup.
- Pump the plunger up and down to build up pressure in the pipe and to remove the blockage.
- If, after a couple of attempts, this has not worked, you will need to look at the sink trap under the sink/basin (probably in a cupboard).
- Put a bucket under the trap and remove the blockage.
  The blockage may come out with the water or you may be able to reach it by exploring the pipe

with a straightened wire coat-hanger (or other piece of reasonably robust wire).
- A really persistent blockage may require you to remove the sink pipe and use the wire to probe further into the depths. Form a small hook on the end to enable you to pull the obstruction out.

TAPS

Dripping taps
This usually means that the washer needs replacing.
- Turn off the water supply to the tap. For a tap fed from the cold water tank, turn off the gate valve or isolating valve in the pipe leading to it. If there isn't one, turn off the main stopcock. Turn on the cold water taps in the bathroom until the flow stops; if dealing with a hot tap, cut off the supply to the hot water cylinder first, then turn it on to drain the hot water cylinder. For a tap fed from the rising main (usually the kitchen tap), turn off the main stopcock and turn on the cold taps until the water flow stops.
- Take off the top of the tap, which will be either screwed or pushed on.
- Unscrew the tap cover, using a cloth to protect the finish if you need to use a spanner.
- Unscrew the large nut (the small one you can also see is holding the packing) and remove the valve mechanism.
- Lift out the washer: the small rubber disc at the base of the valve mechanism.
- Put in the new washer and reverse the previous processes to reassemble the tap.

Supataps
There's no need to turn off the water supply as a valve automatically cuts it off.
- Loosen the top retaining nut (anticlockwise) and hold it with one hand while turning the tap on with the other. When the water flow stops, remove the nozzle.

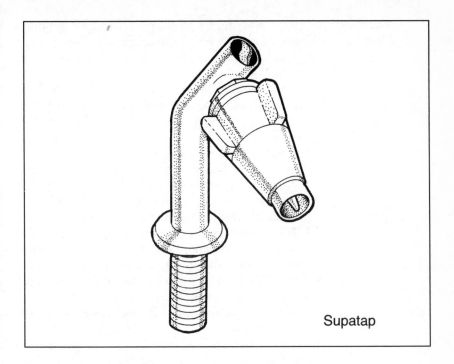

Supatap

- Tap the base of the nozzle against a hard surface and then turn it upside down. The anti-splash device, which contains the washer, should come out.
- Use a screwdriver to extract the washer unit and insert the new one.
- Reassemble the tap.

TOILETS

- Check measurements of fixings at the back and the distance between them before buying a new seat.
- Remove the old bolts holding the fixing assembly. This will probably need several applications of penetrating oil.
- Fit the new seat following the instructions supplied.

Broken seat

Flushing problems Inconsistent flushing is probably caused by the two streams of water which flow around each side of the bowl not meeting in the middle or because of a faulty ball float.

- Remove the lid from the cistern and check that the water is filling to within 2.5cm (1in) of the outlet pipe. If not, adjust the water level by raising the float arm.
- On a Portsmouth valve (by far the most common type) the ballvalve closes a horizontal piston. Adjust the operation of the valve by unscrewing the float from the arm. Then bend the arm slightly upwards and screw the float back on.
- With an equilibrium or a diaphragm valve (both rare), there is no moving piston. Instead, move the adjuster in the appropriate direction.
- If the ball float is leaking, first unscrew it and empty out the water. Screw it back on and tie a plastic bag firmly round it. Buy a new float as soon as possible.
- Stop an overflow as a temporary measure by putting a piece of wood across the top of the cistern (lid removed) and tying the float arm close up to it. Untie to use the toilet and retie immediately afterwards.

Unblocking You will know that a toilet is blocked when water rises to the rim of the bowl and drains away slowly. This usually occurs because something unsuitable has been flushed away. If you have got the kind of toilet down which you really shouldn't flush anything except human excreta, make this crystal clear to your household and any visitors (and supply a bin and plastic bags).

- Wait until the water has drained to its normal level, then throw in a bucketful of water (with force) and flush immediately.
- If this doesn't shift the blockage, take a toilet plunger (from d-i-y stores) and push it firmly down into the bottom of the bowl. Plunge vigorously several times.
- Failing this, call a plumber.

Cutting heating bills

- Lagging • Draught-proofing
- Insulation • Windows
- Replacing the heating system

Using less fuel not only saves money, it's also environmentally friendly. The following tips should help you to cut down your bills in the long term.

LAGGING

It is inexpensive to lag your hot water pipes and lagging will pay for itself in a couple of years. Use either rolls of felt strip, mineral wool lagging or polyurethane foam.

Hot water pipes

Buy a lagging jacket for your hot water tank which conforms to BS 5615. It won't cost much and will recoup its outlay quickly. Fitting it is straight-forward; just follow the instructions supplied.

Hot water tank

Low-income households may be eligible for a grant to help pay for installing certain energy-saving measures. Contact the Energy Action Grants Agency (see **Addresses**) for details.

DRAUGHT-PROOFING

Draught-proofing round windows and doors cuts heating bills and also makes rooms more comfortable to be in. It is a simple d-i-y job, but you may find a confusing array of materials available: covered foam strip or V- or fin-seal are best. Avoid uneven lines which could make closing a door difficult, and don't paint over draught-proofing as it could impair its performance. Fit draught-proofing over the inside of the letter box opening too.

> *Never* draught-proof round a door which leads to a room with a gas fire, boiler or coal fire in it, unless you're sure that there is adequate ventilation, for example via an airbrick.

INSULATION

Loft A quarter of all heat lost in a house escapes through the loft, so insulating your loft could pay for itself within a couple of years. You can call in a professional or do it yourself; it isn't a difficult job but it can be unpleasant. Even if your loft *is* insulated, check it each year as it needs to be topped up if it's dropped below the correct depth (see below).

Materials Materials used include blown mineral wool or cellulose fibre (which need to be installed by a specialist contractor), rolls of mineral wool (d-i-y) or loose-fill vermiculite or pelleted mineral wool (d-i-y).

Protect yourself If you're doing the job yourself, wear protective clothing, rubber gloves and a mask (conforming to BS 6016) as these materials can irritate your skin and throat. *Don't* open the packets until you get into the loft, to avoid spillage, but *do* read the manufacturer's instructions before you start work. Make sure you have enough light to work by and stand on a board while you fit the insulation (not on the ceiling sections between the joists). The total depth of insulation should be 15cm (6in). To find out how much material you need, check the distances between the joists, their length and the number of spaces between the joists. Make sure that the loft is well ventilated so that condensation does not develop.

Loft hatch   Don't forget to insulate the loft hatch by putting draught-proofing round the edges. Bear in mind that after you have insulated the loft the temperature in it will be lower because less heat is being lost, so you'll definitely need to insulate any tanks or pipes in it.

Don't insulate underneath tanks situated on or just above the floor of the loft.

You lose a lot of heat through the uninsulated walls of your home, whether they are solid or cavity-type.

Walls

Cavity   You must hire a professional to insulate your cavity walls (most post-1930s houses have these), but it could cut down heat loss through walls by up to two-thirds. Use a contractor who is a member of the National Cavity Insulation Association or who is registered with the British Standards Institution or the British Board of Agrément (see **Addresses**). There should be little disruption to your home since the material is injected into the wall cavity from outside and the work should take less than a day. Materials that may be used include ureaformaldehyde foam (should conform to BS 5618), mineral wool or polystyrene beads. If your house is timber framed, then cavity insulation is not suitable.

Solid   You can have solid walls insulated from the inside or the outside. External wall insulation must be done by a specialist contractor who is a member of the External Wall Insulation Association (see **Addresses**) and you can select from a range of surface finishes. Note that external insulation can radically alter the appearance of your home and you may need to get planning permission. Your installer should handle this for you if necessary. External insulation is a particularly good idea if your walls are in poor condition and will require work to be done on them in any case.

If you opt for internal insulation, you can do it yourself, but it is a complex job so you might prefer to use a professional. The best method is to build a second internal wall, usually of plasterboard, with an insulating material in the gap between the wall and the plasterboard. Dry lining does make the internal dimensions of the room smaller, and may also involve moving radiators, etc.

Floor   Where a floor is made of concrete or tiles there is little you can do except install fitted flooring and check that any gaps are filled. The best insulator is a good quality carpet over thick felt or rubber underlay, preferably laid on top of a layer of carpet paper. If you have timber floors and you have easy access to the joists, push mineral wool matting or expanded polystyrene boards between them. Or, if access is more difficult, you need to lift the floorboards and put mineral wool between them.

- Staple flexible netting across the joists so that it hangs down in each space like a hammock.
- Put the mineral wool into the 'hammocks' and replace the floorboards.
- Don't block up any airbricks or you will get dampness and rot.
- Fill any gaps between the floor and skirting-boards using either a mastic gun or quadrant beading (a quartered length of round dowel rod, bought ready-cut, which fits snugly into the angle between the floor and skirting-board).

WINDOWS

With double glazing, a layer of air is trapped between two panes of glass. Because this air doesn't mix with either the inside or the outside air it acts as an insulating barrier and also, to some extent, reduces outside noise. It also makes it more comfortable to sit near windows, especially bay windows which are otherwise cold in winter. Good quality double glazing is not cheap and is only worth considering if your windows need replacing. It also helps to prevent condensation.

Double glazing

Aluminium or metal frames are fitted inside your existing windows. They can be hinged or sliding, so can be opened when you open the outside window. This is a cheaper method which you can fit yourself and, because the savings are about the same in terms of heat loss as having double glazing, it is more cost-effective.

Secondary glazing

This form of double glazing (d-i-y or professional) comes direct from the factory with the glass already in a frame which needs to be fitted into your existing window space. It is an effective measure against condensation but if fitting it yourself, you must be careful not to damage the seal.

Hermetically sealed glazing

A cheap but effective method of d-i-y double glazing is to use cling film, stretched across the window frame and made taut by applying heat from a hair-dryer to it. This works well and can be taken off in summer and replaced cheaply when necessary. Sheets of rigid plastic could also be fixed to the glass with double-sided tape or magnetic strips.

D-i-y

Lined and interlined curtains will reduce heat loss when drawn. But make sure that curtains don't cover radiators, which will prevent heat getting into the room. If you're out all day and would like your

Curtains

curtains drawn before you come home, an electric drawing system with a time switch could be the answer. Blinds and shutters will also help to keep the heat in.

REPLACING YOUR HEATING SYSTEM

Old systems can be inefficient and may lead to higher bills. You may need to replace your boiler and install modern controls which will produce heat in specific areas at specific times. A seven-day timer can be programmed to adjust the time when heating goes on and off and can allow for workdays and weekends, and a room thermostat works by keeping different rooms at different maximum temperatures.

Cylinder thermostat   This is quite cheap and can be fitted to your hot water cylinder. It saves money by controlling the temperature of your hot water.

Thermostatic radiator valves   These are also worth investing in. They allow you to control the temperature of each room separately, and are especially worthwhile if you live in a large house where some rooms are used less than others. By keeping some rooms at a lower heat, rather than unheated, the risk of dampness is also reduced.

Low-income households may be eligible for a grant to help pay for installing certain energy-saving measures. Contact the Energy Action Grants Agency (see **Addresses**) for details.

TIPS FOR CUTTING FUEL BILLS

- Put aluminium foil (shiny side inwards) on the walls behind radiators to prevent heat being lost through the outside walls.
- Put shelves above radiators to help deflect heat back into the room. These are particularly good where radiators are located under windows.
- Use sausage-shaped draught excluders against doors where you can't fit draught-proofing.
- Turn down the thermostat on the hot water cylinder (and on your central heating thermostat) by a couple of degrees. The difference will be barely noticeable but it could save up to 10 per cent of the fuel you use in heating.
- Shower instead of bathing; five showers cost the same as one bath.
- If you are thinking about changing your heating system, it may be worthwhile considering changing fuels.
- Think about appliances which are on standby; turning off the TV and video at night and not using the clock on the microwave, if possible, could save you more than you think.
- Fit energy-saving light-bulbs. Compact fluor-escent light-bulbs (CFLs) are more expensive to buy but last longer and are cheaper to run.
- Don't run the washing-machine or dishwasher until you have a full load. Run them at the lowest temperature that's suitable for what's being washed.
- Put lids on pans when cooking.
- Try not to use the oven for just one dish.

3

SAFETY FIRST

Fire safety
Accidents at home
Well secured

Fire safety

- Precautions   • Fire drill
- When fire breaks out   • Household fires

Fire can result in serious injury or death. Therefore it is vital to organise safety precautions and to ensure that all members of the household know what to do in the event of a fire.

PRECAUTIONS

- Fit smoke detectors on each floor of your home. In a big house you may need more than one on each floor.
- Install a fire blanket in the kitchen.
- Fit self-closing hinges to doors, especially if your home is a high-fire risk, with a thatched roof or of clapboard design, for example.
- If there are smokers in the home, always make sure that there are ashtrays around. A cigarette is safer there than smouldering dangerously on the arm of a chair.
- Keep aerosol cans away from sources of heat.
- Be careful when using d-i-y products which are flammable. Work in well-ventilated conditions and don't smoke. Store flammable liquids in a cool airy place, not near hot water pipes or in a place such as an understair cupboard where a fire could cut off an escape route. Don't store newspapers under stairs.
- Make sure everyone in the house knows a choice of escape routes if the obvious one is blocked.

Daily checks   Check the house last thing at night, especially if there are smokers or an open fire has been lit.
Make sure that there is nothing flammable within reach of a naked flame.

112

Don't forget that a pilot light is a naked flame.
Make sure that the cooker is switched off after use.
Ensure that keys to doors and windows are accessible in case you need to get out in a hurry.

FIRE DRILL

- Hold a fire practice from time to time so that all members of the household know what to do, where to find keys and alternative ways of vacating a home.
- Make sure that everyone knows where the nearest telephone box/neighbour's telephone is and the procedure for calling the fire service (see below).
- Don't expect people (particularly children and the elderly) to be able to climb out of windows or perform other acrobatic feats. Impress on them that it is better to shut the door, open a window and call for help than to attempt a dangerous manoeuvre.

WHEN FIRE BREAKS OUT

- Don't aim to be a hero. Unless you can control the fire (see below), get everyone out as fast as possible.
- Call the fire service from a neighbour's phone. Dial 999 and ask for 'Fire'. Give your address clearly and state whether people are trapped on an upper floor.
- Don't be tempted to go back into the blaze to rescue pets or valuables.
- Remember, fumes from burning items such as foam-filled furniture kill as easily as flames.

- Don't panic.
- Go to a room as far away as possible from the fire and with the best chance of calling for help (i.e. street side of the house rather than garden side).

If trapped by fire

113

- Keep low to avoid being choked by the smoke – which is less dense near floor level.
- Shut the door and block the gap at the bottom with a rug, piece of bedding, garment or towel. If possible, wet the item first.
- Shout down the street for help.
- Don't jump unless it's the only course of action that will save your life.

HOUSEHOLD FIRES

Chimney/
fireplace
- Use water on a fireplace fire but call the fire service if a chimney is alight.
- Shut down any ventilation to the fireplace and close doors and windows.
- Pull furniture and carpets away from the fireplace.

> Have chimneys swept regularly so that soot does not build up. Check fires before going to bed and always leave a fireguard in position.

Chip-pan/
frying-pan
- Turn off the cooker if you can reach it.
- Cover the pan either with a fire blanket, a damp (i.e. wrung out) tea towel or a large lid or plate.
- Leave until cool.
DO NOT THROW WATER ON IT.

Clothes
- Attempt to lie yourself or the victim down to prevent flames reaching the head or face.
- Wrap the victim in a rug, blanket, curtain, thick coat or other heavy piece of fabric (but not one made of synthetic fibres, which will stick to burns and is dangerous/difficult to remove).

- Pour water or another non-flammable liquid on the flames.
- Treat minor burns (see **Accidents at home** section) or get medical attention.

Electrical appliance

- Unplug the appliance or switch off the electricity at the mains.
- Use water to douse the flames on small appliances but not on a TV or computer for which you should use a fire blanket or piece of heavy fabric. TVs and computers retain a residual current.

DO NOT USE AN APPLIANCE OR SOCKET AGAIN UNTIL IT HAS BEEN CHECKED BY A QUALIFIED ELECTRICIAN.

Foam furniture

- Shut the door to prevent the fumes from spreading.
- Evacuate the home.
- Call the fire service

FUMES FROM FOAM-FILLED FURNITURE CAN KILL IN LESS THAN TWO MINUTES.

- Try to make sure that all new foam-filled furniture you buy is made from fire-resistant materials.

Oil heater

Throw water on the flames but stand at least 6ft away so that they can't reach you. (If in any doubt, use a fire blanket instead.)

- Close the door if you have to leave the room to refill the water container.

Accidents at home

- Eliminating hazards   • Be prepared
  • Treating accidents at home

Most accidents in the home can be prevented by making your home as safe as possible, particularly if your household includes elderly people or children.

ELIMINATE HAZARDS

Go round your home, room by room, looking for possible hazards and then deal with them.

Glass doors   Internal doors with glass panels should be fitted with safety or laminated glass which stays in place if shattered and does not produce shards and splinters.

Trailing flexes   Get rid of trailing flexes. If necessary, fit, or get an electrician to fit, a new socket outlet nearer to the item being powered. Note that it is not safe to run a trailing flex under a rug or carpet as it might overheat and cause a fire.

Socket outlets   An overloaded socket outlet, with adaptors running several electrical items off one socket, can cause a fire. Fit extra socket outlets. To reduce the risk of a fatal electric shock, fit a residual current device (RCD), which monitors the current passing along the live wire and will isolate a faulty circuit.

Empty socket outlets should be filled with plug covers (from children's retailers) to prevent sharp items or fingers being pushed into them.

Unguarded fires, including flame-effect models, which can get very hot, need a guard if there are children around. Always place a fireguard in front of an open fire when there is no one around.

Unguarded fires

Loose rugs can cause people to trip. Buy special anti-slip products to hold them in place or remove rugs altogether from busy parts of the house.

Loose rugs

An unsecured stair carpet can cause people to trip. Fix it firmly in position and make sure there are no loose threads.

Stair carpet

This can result in accidents, so make sure that busy areas of the house and stairs are well lit. Where people need to use rooms at night, for example, the bathroom, fit low-level lighting at strategic points and have it on a time-switch.

Poor lighting

Make sure these are kept in locked cupboards or well out of the reach of children at all times. Harmful substances include cleaning products (which, even if not deadly, can cause vomiting and illness) and medicines. *Never* decant them out of their original containers. Medicines which are no longer required should be taken to a pharmacist for disposal. Remember that garden sheds often contain poisonous substances, so keep them locked.

Poisonous substances

Sharp tools and knives should be kept in a safe place, not only out of reach of children, but where you won't cut your hand when reaching for them (see also **Food and the kitchen** section).

Tools and knives

Keep your windows locked, especially if there are children in the house. Make sure you know where the key is kept.

Windows

Safety points   Constant vigilance is *vital* where vulnerable people are at risk. Make sure you:

- *don't* leave hot drinks lying around where they could be knocked over and scald someone
- *don't* allow saucepan handles to protrude over the front of the cooker
- *don't* leave matches and lighters lying around
- *don't* leave the iron switched on and unattended
- *don't* leave ladders and steps lying around
- *do* switch off the toaster at the socket
- *do* be careful when undertaking tasks that are intrinsically dangerous, such as boiling jam, painting a ceiling, changing a light-bulb and so on
- *do* fit safety gates to keep children out of hazardous areas, such as the kitchen and at the top *and* bottom of the stairs, to prevent them from falling.

BE PREPARED

Assemble a first-aid kit in a lidded box and make sure that each adult in the house knows where it is kept (it is also sensible to keep a small first-aid kit in the car and to take one with you when you go on holiday). Consider attending a first-aid course which will give you more skills and confidence when coping with accidents. Courses are available around the country, run by The St John Ambulance and The British Red Cross (see **Addresses**).

Calling an   A serious accident requires professional medical
ambulance   attention quickly with no time to wait for a doctor's surgery session. If you don't feel it's advisable or safe to take someone to a hospital Accident and Emergency Department in a car, call an ambulance, which carries medical equipment to ease the trauma of the journey.
Procedure   Dial 999 and ask for 'Ambulance' – you do *not* require coins if calling from a pay phone. While waiting for the ambulance, take any

BASIC FIRST-AID KIT

- paracetemol for painkilling
- antihistamine cream for insect bites and stings
- bandages for sprains
- plasters for cuts
- blunt-edged scissors for cutting bandages and plasters
- safety pins for fastening bandages
- gauze for cleaning cuts and grazes
- sterile dressings
- sterile eye dressings
- triangular bandage for making a sling
- tweezers for removing splinters.

necessary precautionary measures (see below). Bear in mind that in heavy traffic at busy times of day it may take some time for the ambulance to arrive.
If the ambulance does not turn up within a reasonable period of time and you are concerned for the person, keep redialling the ambulance service.

TREATING ACCIDENTS AT HOME

It is essential to practise artificial respiration (the 'kiss of life') if someone has stopped breathing, since brain damage may occur after three minutes without oxygen. The procedure is as follows.
- Lie the person down.

Artificial respiration

- Put your hands on the forehead and chin and tilt the head back to open the windpipe and clear the air passage.
- If there is an obstruction in the mouth, use two fingers to remove it.
- Keeping the head tilted back, pinch the nose between your thumb and forefinger, place your lips over the person's mouth and blow in two long breaths to make the chest rise.
- Unseal your mouth while the chest falls.
- If there is a pulse, continue sealing the mouth and blowing every four or five seconds until breathing starts again.
- Once breathing has started, put the person into the **recovery position** (see page 127).

Bandaging While minor cuts can usually be covered with a sufficiently large plaster, deep cuts should be covered with a sterile dressing – an absorbent pad with a bandage attached.

- Start bandaging about three turns below the cut, keeping the tension even. Finish two or three turns above the cut. Fasten with a safety pin.
- Use an appropriate width of bandage: narrow for fingers and toes; wider for arms and legs.
- Use a crêpe bandage for a sprain, applied in a figure-of-eight around both sides of the joint.
- For an emergency bandage, use a clean handkerchief.

Bleeding
- Lie the person down and remove clothing from around the wound.
- Raise the wound above the level of the heart to reduce bleeding.
- If there is nothing embedded in the wound, cover it with a piece of gauze and press down hard, squeezing the sides together gently.
- Keep pressing for between five and fifteen minutes, adding further layers of cloth or paper (but not removing the original ones).
- In all instances of major bleeding, call an ambulance.

- Where an **object is embedded in the wound**, leave it in as a plug.
- Put a piece of clean cloth over the wound.
- Form two sausage-shaped pads out of gauze, put them around the wound and bandage gently into position, taking care not to push on the embedded object.
- Get the person to a hospital Accident and Emergency Department.

Broken bones

- Treat *stopped breathing* and *unconsciousness* before anything else.
- Avoid moving the person, if possible.
- If a person's legs are broken, call an ambulance; if the arms are broken you may be able to take the person to hospital in a car.
- Secure the arm to the body with bandages, stockings or tights under which you have placed some form of padding.
- Make the person as comfortable as possible without too much movement, supporting the injured limb with cushions, rolled blankets or clothes.

Breathing (stopped)

Apply **artificial respiration** (see page 119).

Burns and scalds

All, except minor burns, require medical attention. It is essential to cool all burns thoroughly before further treatment and to remove jewellery while the affected part is under water, unless there is swelling which prevents this.

- Remove the person from the source of the burn, taking care not to hurt yourself in the process.
- If the source is electrical, switch the power off at the mains or pull out the plug, holding the insulated flex as you tug. If this can't be done, push the person with a wooden pole (broom handle, garden tool handle – but keep metal parts clear). Do *not* touch the person until this is done.
- Run **minor burns** under cool water for at least ten minutes or until the pain lessens. This prevents

the burn from continuing to 'cook'.

- Cover the burn with a dry sterile dressing or clean handkerchief. Do not apply any cream or ointment.
- With a **severe burn,** first remove any jewellery and loosen clothing but do *not* remove anything which is sticking to the burn.
- Raise burned arms or legs above heart level to reduce blood flow to them.
- Apply cool water to the affected area.
- Cover with a sterile dressing (or clean sheet or pillowcase for a large area).
- With **electrical burns**, be ready to treat *stopped breathing* or *shock*.
- Hold **chemical burns** under cool running water for at least ten minutes. Remove any affected clothing as you rinse, taking care not to get chemical contamination on the person or yourself.
- Where **clothing is on fire**, attempt to lie the person down to prevent flames reaching the head or face. Wrap the person in a rug, blanket, curtain, thick coat or other heavy piece of fabric (not made from synthetic fibres which will stick to the burn). Pour water or other non-flammable liquid on the flame.

Choking

- Remove any loose obstructions (including false teeth) from the mouth.
- Try to make the person cough.
- Bend the person over, with the head lower than the chest, and slap firmly between the shoulder blades with the heel of your hand. One slap could remove the blockage; don't do this more than four or five times.

If this does not remove the blockage.

- Stand behind the person, clench your fist (with the thumb outside) and put it – thumb-side inwards – between the navel and the bottom of the breastbone.

- Hold the clenched fist with your other hand and pull firmly with your elbows going upwards and backwards up to a maximum of four times.

- Call an ambulance if both methods fail.

- Wash the wound with soap and warm water.
- Cover with a clean dry dressing.
- See a doctor for a tetanus injection.

Dog bites

- If necessary, apply **artificial respiration** (see page 119) and, if breathing starts, place the person in the **recovery position** (see page 127).
- Call an ambulance.
- Do *not* induce vomiting.
- Save pills, the bottle or container plus a sample of vomit to help the doctor to identify the drug.

Drug overdose

- Get the person away from the source of the electricity (see **Electric burns** in **Burns and scalds** above).
- Call an ambulance.
- If necessary, give **artificial respiration** (see page 119) then place in the **recovery position** (see page 127).
- Cool the burn, then cover it with a dry sterile dressing or clean cloth.

Electric shock

- When convulsions occur, help the person to avoid injuring himself or herself on the furniture.
- Loosen the clothing around the neck.
- Check if the person carries any emergency information on a card or bracelet and follow the instructions supplied.
- Do *not* put anything in the person's mouth.
- When convulsions are over, place the person in the **recovery position** (see page 127). He or she may be unconscious for a while. If this lasts for more than 15 minutes, call medical help.

Epileptic fit

Eye injuries *Chemical burns* A chemical burn to the eye needs to be flushed with running water from a tap or jug for at least ten minutes.

- Pat dry gently and cover with a clean dressing.
- Go to a hospital Accident and Emergency Department.

Glass or other sharp object If you have glass or any other sharp object lodged in the eye, this will need immediate medical attention.

- Call an ambulance.
- In the meantime, protect the eye by taping a disposable paper or plastic cup over it. Cover the other eye with a bandage or patch so the person keeps both eyes as still as possible.
- Accompany the person to hospital.

Grit To remove grit, draw the eyelid away from the eyeball and get the person to roll the eye up and down and from side to side to reveal where the grit is sited. Don't let the person rub the eye.

- Bend the head towards the injured side and run lukewarm water over the eyeball. Alternatively, get the person to put his or her face into a basin of water and blink underwater.
- Grit embedded in the eyelid can be removed by rolling the eyelid up over a matchstick, holding the lashes, then using the dampened corner of a clean handkerchief to dislodge the grit.

Fainting People who are about to faint may appear to be sweating a lot, have cold, clammy skin, become pale and yawn a lot. To prevent fainting, lie the person down or sit him or her with the head between the knees.

When someone has fainted:

- lie him or her on the back and raise the legs above the level of the head
- loosen clothing and ventilate the room well.

If consciousness does not return within a few minutes, place the person in the **recovery position** (see page 127). When conscious, keep the person resting for a few minutes and check for any injuries which may have occurred if the person fell.

(See **Food and the kitchen** section – pages 10-11.) *Food poisoning*

(See **Broken bones** on page 121.) *Fractures*

Frostbite

- Get the person into shelter and remove clothing and jewellery in contact with the affected area.
- Warm the skin slowly using your hands and body. Do *not* rub or apply intense heat.
- If blood-filled blisters appear as circulation returns, take care not to break them and do not treat them.
- Wrap the frostbitten part in a clean cloth, such as a pillowcase or sheet, and cover it with a coat or blanket.
- Take the person to hospital.

Head injury

Any head injury may result in a fractured skull or concussion. Symptoms may include bleeding, bruising, drowsiness, confusion, memory loss, headache and vomiting.
- Arrange for an ambulance to take the person to a hospital Accident and Emergency Department.

Heart attack

If you suspect a heart attack, help the person into the most comfortable position, usually a half-seated position (lying back, propped up with pillows). Support the head with pillows and place another under the knees.
- Call an ambulance.
- Loosen clothing.
- Keep the person still and don't supply food or drink.
- If loss of consciousness occurs, place the person in the **recovery position** (see page 127).
- If breathing stops, apply **artificial respiration** (see page 119).

Heat exhaustion

Symptoms may include cramp, dizziness, headache and sickness. Speedy treatment is important.
- Put the person in a cool, shady place and remove all but light clothing.

- If the person's temperature is above normal (37°C/98.4°F), he or she may be suffering from heat stroke (see below).
- Replace lost fluids with a drink to which you have added a quarter teaspoon (1.5ml) salt per 500ml. Give it in small quantities every ten minutes.
- If loss of consciousness occurs, place the person in the **recovery position** (see opposite).

Heat stroke Heat stroke (sun stroke) is more serious than heat exhaustion and is caused when heat can not escape from the body.

- Put the person in a cool area and remove clothing.
- Wrap the person in sheets or towels soaked in cold water and fan him or her until the body temperature drops to normal (37°C/98.4°F).
- Call a doctor or ambulance.
- If unconscious, place the person in the **recovery position** (see below).
- Give the person a warm, sweet drink such as tea, but *no* alcohol.

Insect bites/ stings These are usually painful, rather than dangerous, but can be fatal if the person has an allergic reaction or is bitten in the throat or mouth. If so, you should take the person to the Accident and Emergency Department immediately.

Otherwise, with bee stings, remove the sting with tweezers, a knife or a fingernail. Ant, bee, midge, mosquito and wasp stings may be treated with antihistamine cream (first ascertain that the patient isn't allergic to it).

Dislocated joints
- Make the person comfortable.
- Support the dislocated joint with cushions, pillows or rolled blankets or clothing.
- Call an ambulance or take the person to the Accident and Emergency Department.

- Loosen clothing around the neck.
- Seat the person and get him or her to bend the head forward over a bowl to catch drips of blood. He or she should then pinch the nostrils together for at least ten minutes while breathing through the mouth.
- If bleeding stops, sit quietly and avoid blowing the nose.
- If bleeding recurs, repeat the treatment for ten minutes.
- If bleeding persists, see a doctor.

Nosebleed

(See **Dog bites** on page 123.)

Pet bites

Symptoms may include stomach pains, vomiting, diarrhoea, convulsions, delirium and breathing difficulties.

Poisoning

- Call an ambulance.
- If the person is unconscious, put him or her in the **recovery position** (see below).
- If breathing stops, apply **artificial respiration** (see page 119).
- If the poison is something like bleach, which burns, give milk or water slowly to dilute it. (Do *not* give drinks if the person has swallowed a non-corrosive poison.)
- Do *not* induce vomiting.
- Try to find a sample of the poison (or the container) and give this, with a sample of vomit, to the doctor.

- Ensure the person is on his or her back.
- Open the airway. Place the arm nearest to you at right angles to the body, elbow bent, palm uppermost.
- Bring the other arm across and hold the hand against the chest.
- Grasp the thigh furthest from you and pull the knee up, keeping the foot flat on the ground.
- Keeping the hand against the chest, pull on the thigh to roll the casualty towards you, resting his or her head upon the outstretched hand.

Recovery position

- Tilt the head back to open the airway. Adjust the hand under the cheek to ensure the airway is open.
- Adjust the leg so that the hip and knee are at right angles.

Shock Symptoms may include pale, clammy skin, restlessness and anxiety, weak, rapid or irregular pulse, dizziness, faintness, blurred vision, sickness, chill and thirst.

- Call a doctor or ambulance immediately.
- Lie the person on his or her back.
- Prop the legs about 20cm (8in) off the ground on cushions to direct blood to the brain.
- Apply any appropriate first aid.
- Loosen clothing.
- Cover the person with a coat or blanket.
- Moisten the person's lips with water if required, but do *not* give food or drink in case an anaesthetic is required.
- Keep the person still.
- If breathing stops, apply **artificial respiration** (see page 119).
- If loss of consciousness occurs, put the person in the **recovery position** (see above).

Splinters
- Wash your hands and sterilise a pair of tweezers by passing them through a flame or by boiling them in water for ten minutes.
- Clean the skin around the splinter with soap and warm water, wiping *away* from the wound.
- Dry the area and use the tweezers to extract the splinter (using a magnifying glass if it's difficult to see).
- Wash the area and cover with a plaster.

If a splinter is large, deeply embedded, won't come out or breaks, go to a doctor.

- Remove the shoe if an ankle is sprained.
- Place the wrist or ankle above the level of the head.
- Apply a cold compress.
- Bandage the sprain firmly in a figure-of-eight movement.

Sprains

- Raise the injury above the level of the head.
- Apply a cold compress.
- Bandage firmly, but not too tightly, in case of swelling.
- Support a strained arm in a sling.

Strains

Symptoms may include headache, paralysis on one side, difficulty in speaking and confusion.
- Call an ambulance.
- Lie the person down with his or her head and shoulders raised slightly on a pillow.
- Tilt the head to one side so the saliva can drain out of the mouth.
- Loosen clothing.
- Do *not* give food or drink.
- If loss of consciousness occurs, place in the **recovery position** (see page 127).

Stroke

- Save a **whole** tooth that's been knocked out in case it can be replaced.
- Put the tooth back in the hole or put it in a cup of milk (if there's a danger that a child may swallow it), then go to the dentist.
- Remove a piece of **broken** tooth from the mouth with the fingers.
- Sit the person with his or her head bent forward over a bowl until the bleeding has stopped.
- Visit a dentist to have the teeth and gums checked as soon as possible.

Teeth knocked out/broken

- Put the person in the **recovery position** (see page 127).
- If breathing stops, carry out **artificial respiration** (see page 119).

Un-consciousness

- Return the person to the recovery position once breathing restarts.
- Loosen clothing.
- Call an ambulance.

Vomiting
- Get medical help if there is blood in vomit, if vomiting continues for more than four hours or if it occurs along with diarrhoea or cramp.
- Get the person to rest and drink plenty of water to prevent dehydration.
- When the person feels better, offer weak tea or a light, clear soup followed by light meals consisting of non-greasy foods.

Well secured

- Vulnerable areas   • Security tips
- Be alarmed

Making your home as secure as possible should deter the casual thief. A really determined burglar will always find a way in, but most thefts are committed by opportunists who see an open window or handy ladder to gain access to a rooftop skylight.

VULNERABLE AREAS

Identify the vulnerable points in and around your home. The Crime Prevention Officer at your local police station will provide free advice on this, as well as advising you on the best methods of security for your needs. The areas listed below are the most important to protect.

Garden

Low or broken fences offer access, as does a wall with handy footholds. Plant prickly shrubs or a hedge and install security lighting if your garden is dark and shady enough to provide cover for an intruder (though bear in mind that local wildlife will probably set it off). Take particular care to lock windows which could be reached from a neighbouring tree branch.

Drainpipes

Drainpipes are a cinch for the agile thief. Coat the drainpipes with special anti-climb paint which will keep them permanently slippery and will leave a deposit on the hands and clothes of anyone attempting to scale them. Make sure that all windows near drainpipes are fitted with locks.

Shed and garage   Keep your shed and garage locked at all times when not in use, since they are likely to contain tools which could be handy for breaking windows or doors. If your ladder is too long to be stored in your shed or garage, fit it firmly to an outside wall with locked bolts. If the garage has a connecting door to the house, this should always be kept locked.

Back gate   Make sure that your back gate is strong and locked at all times. Some barbed wire along the top will act as a deterrent.

Back alley   Get together with neighbours on both sides and arrange to fit strong lockable gates at both ends of the alley. If it's used for refuse collection, you will have to come to some arrangement about unlocking the gates at the appropriate time.

Back and side doors   Back and side doors should have similar locks (i.e. just as strong) to the front door (see below).

Windows   Don't be tempted to leave windows open while you're out, even in summer and even if you'll only be out for a short time.
French (and patio doors) Should be made of toughened or laminated glass which cracks but doesn't shatter when attacked. The doors should have locks at the top and bottom (so that they can't be lifted out if the glass is broken) and a good lock where they join.
Louvred Removing the slats of a louvred window is fairly easy, so glue them into place with epoxy resin or fit a special louvre lock. The best solution is to replace louvred glass with a single pane, which will open if necessary, and fit it with a window lock.

Front door   *Locks* To protect your front door install two locks: a deadlocked rim latch which snaps into the lock keep as the door is closed, locking automatically and a five-lever mortise lock which you must 'throw' with a key. Keep the mortise locked if you are in a much-burgled area and, in any case, always lock it at night. Locks Kitemarked to BS 3621 are the strongest.

Glass panels   These should be toughened or backed with a wrought-iron door grille.

Screening   Some form of screening for callers may make you feel safer. In houses, fit a spy hole or a strong chain so that you can open the door a few inches to identify the caller. Front doors of flats may be inferior to the main front door so, if this is the case, replace yours with a sturdier version and good locks, since it is easy for a would-be thief to enter the main front door accompanying another resident or posing as a service engineer or meter reader. Always check the identity of anyone calling unexpectedly. People representing services such as the electricity company or social services will carry identity cards; if they don't, leave them outside while you telephone their organisation.

SECURITY TIPS

Keys

All your locks will be in vain if keys to them are widely available. Be careful whom you entrust with the keys to your home and never leave a key under a flowerpot or on a string inside the letterbox flap. Never leave a key in the lock, especially on the inside of a door with a glass panel.

Don't allow anyone who doesn't live in your home to have door keys except, possibly, a trusted neighbour (useful if you forget your keys) or cleaner etc. Bear in mind that completely honest people who work in your home may have friends and relations who are less trustworthy – and who know they have a key. If anyone loses their keys, you must change the locks if the keys could be identified – if, for example, a handbag was stolen. Don't put your address, phone number of any other form of identification on your key ring.

On holiday   Remember to cancel the milk and newspapers and ask a neighbour to remove any post or free newspapers that might be left in the door.

Out of sight   Don't advertise the fact that you own things worth stealing. Avoid keeping CD-players, computers, stereos, TVs, video recorders, valuable ornaments and pictures etc. where they might be seen by passers-by. If you are in a very exposed position, put up net curtains to act as a barrier to viewing.

Lights on   Leaving a light on when you're out is a good idea. You may also want to invest in a security light or time-switch which is designed to turn lights on and off at intervals – especially useful if you're going on holiday.

Locking up   Different types of doors and windows need different types of lock. Your Crime Prevention Officer will tell you which kinds are the most easy to install by yourself. If you need a locksmith to do the job, ask the officer to recommend one used regularly by the police.

BE ALARMED

A burglar alarm is a deterrent to thieves and it can give you further peace of mind. There are two main types of alarm.

Bell only   If choosing a bell-only alarm, make sure it is good and loud. Anything below 95 decibels is unlikely to be effective, either in scaring a burglar away or alerting the neighbours. Make sure too that the alarm will switch itself off after a reasonable period of time (say, 30 minutes), as a longer period of ringing is unlikely to get more of a reaction (and it will mean your neighbours will have little sympathy the next time it goes off).

If you live in an area where no one will hear an alarm, install one which is wired into the local monitoring centre or police station. These cost more but bring immediate help and are sensible fitments if a home contains many valuables, if the area has a low domestic population or if the homeowner is infirm and concerned about break-ins. Alarms may be triggered by magnetic switches on doors and windows or pressure pads under mats or carpets. An acoustic alarm will ring at the sound of a door or window being opened; an infra-red or ultrasonic alarm is triggered by the body heat of an intruder.

Monitored

Some alarms require wiring, others do not. Whichever type of alarm you install, make sure it won't be set off by pets moving around the home. Make sure too that windows and doors are securely fixed so that a draught won't cause them to move as if they were being opened.

A cheaper solution is to fit an alarm box that has no bell and is not wired up. This may act as a deterrent against an opportunist burglar.

Other alternatives

Or consider a system with a panic button which enables *you* to set off the alarm if you think there are intruders in the house. If in a bedroom, it should be within easy reach of where you lie in bed; another useful place is by the front or the back door. Most systems can take more than one panic button.

Burglar alarms can be set to operate after a specific period of time. This allows *you* to get out of the house before the alarm thinks *you're* the burglar. Time yourself doing this manoeuvre so that you know how long you'll need.

You can install an alarm yourself or have it installed by a professional. If you're having it installed by an outside company it's worth finding out if the company is recognised by the National Approval Council for Security Systems (see **Addresses**) who will check that both bell-only and monitored alarms confirm to BS 4737.

Installation

TEN POINTS TO REMEMBER IF THERE'S A BREAK-IN

- If you arrive home and sense or see that someone is in the house, *don't* go in. Go to a neighbour's house and call the police.

- If you wake up to a noise, use the panic button. Put on the lights in your bedroom. Make a noise (if you're alone, talk as if there were two of you). Call the police.

- Most casual burglars will take the chance to escape if disturbed.

- If you must confront an intruder, *don't* use undue force. You can use reasonable force but if you injure someone it's possible he or she may sue you. If you get the chance, try to memorise his or her appearance.

- If you are attacked or raped, call the police as soon as you can. *Don't* wash and *don't* change your clothes.

- If you have been burgled, don't touch anything. Wait until the police give you the go-ahead to do so.

- Make a note of any damage and, if possible, photograph the scene.

- List what has been taken.

- Inform your insurance company.

- Make temporary security arrangements. If you don't have reliable contacts, ask the police for the names of carpenters, glaziers and locksmiths.

4

OUTSIDE THE HOME

External problems
Cycles and cars
Neighbours

External problems

- Be prepared • Airbricks
- Damp-proof courses • Doors
- Drains • Fences and gates
- Gutters • Paths and patios
- Roofs • Steps
- Walls • Windows

Keep regular checks on the outside of your property so you can spot when things start to go wrong and sort them out before a full-scale repair by a professional is needed.

BE PREPARED

There are various ways of keeping a check. One is to get a pair of binoculars and, standing some distance away, scan the home thoroughly to spot any cracks, damp or other problems. You should also keep a vigilant eye indoors for tell-tale signs of dampness on walls of draughts whistling through window frames.

Ladders Provided you have a head for heights, you should use a ladder to check gutters, drainpipes and chimney-stacks. Be careful when using a ladder or you may have an accident.

Check the ladder for strength and safety. If it has loose wooden rungs, buy a new ladder. If you're using any kind of ladder on soft ground, put down a wide solid board to rest the legs on and to prevent them from sinking. Always position a ladder so that the distance between its feet and the wall is about one-quarter of the total ladder length; any nearer and it might come away from the wall. Fix it to firm supports at the sides and bottom if possible; otherwise, secure it when you reach the top. Do not rely on someone else holding it steady for you and do not go up at all if the wind is strong. Note that a worktower (which you can hire if you can't store one) is a more robust and confidence-giving piece of equipment from which to work off the ground.

- If you are taking several tools or bulky equipment up with you, use a ladder tray to hold them or wear a tool belt.
- A ladder stand-off is useful when you don't want the ladder to lean against something which it could damage, such as guttering.
- Don't go up a ladder unless there is someone within shouting distance in case you need help.

AIRBRICKS

Airbricks provide under-floor ventilation to homes that have suspended timber floors and prevent damp from entering at floor level and creating rotten timbers and dampness.

Maintenance

- Airbricks should be kept clear at all times: use a thin bamboo cane to poke through the holes from time to time to check that there are no obstructions.
- Airbricks can cause draughts in the home. Prevent this by putting down fitted floorcovering or sealing the gaps between floorboards and skirting.

DAMP-PROOF COURSES

Damp-proof coursing is designed to prevent damp from rising up the walls. A damp-proof course usually runs around the outside walls, about 15cm (6in) above ground level. It is vital that nothing touches the course or it will allow damp into the home. Check regularly that earth, stones, foliage, etc. have not built up to a level where they can 'bridge' the damp course.

DOORS

Banging doors   If you have to leave a door open, perhaps to keep a check on small children, use a rubber or plastic doorstop to prevent draughts from causing it to bang against the wall behind. Either screw the stop to the wall or floor or fit it on the back of the door itself. If it is the handle that is damaging the wall, fit a stop that projects beyond its depth – you may need to use a small block of wood to do this.

Rattling doors   Remove the striker plate (the insert in the door frame where the latch fits). Unscrew this and cut the recess back a small distance towards the door stop. Refit the striker plate and check that the rattling has stopped. If not, move the striker plate a fraction more until you are successful.

Sticking doors   Plane down the door to fit the door frame, then remove a further 3mm to ensure it will still swing even if humidity in the air causes the wood to swell. Prime the bare wood, then paint or seal. Fit a flexible draught-proofing strip to the bottom of the door which will ensure it is a good fit whether the wood is swollen or contracted.

DRAINS

Blocked drains occur most often inside the house. To clear inside drains see **Unblocking sinks** and **Unblocking toilets** in the **Plumbing** section.

Keep external drains clear by pouring neat household bleach or a solution of washing soda and hot water down them once a week.

Locating the blockage

To clear an external drain, lift the manhole cover nearest the blockage. If it is full of water, the blockage is further along the system; if empty, the blockage will be between the first and second manholes. Continue inspecting manholes until you either (a) locate the blockage or (b) reach the last manhole on your property, after which it is the responsibility of the water company.

Removing the blockage

To remove a blockage on your property you need to hire or borrow a set of drain rods. These screw together to the required length and take plunger and corkscrew head attachments.

- Whilst wearing protective gloves and using the corkscrew head, insert three or four rods which you have screwed together into the drain and turn clockwise (turning anticlockwise will unscrew them). Once you reach the blockage and attack it, the water will start to flow again and dislodge the blockage.

- Remove the rods (still turning clockwise) and replace the corkscrew head with the plunger. Turn on the kitchen and bathroom taps and apply the plunger to the opening of the drain to shift any remaining debris.

- Before replacing the manhole cover, clean round the edge and apply a thick coating of car grease to make a good fit.

- If you can't face doing any of this – or aren't strong or agile enough – call in a professional drain-cleaning firm. Look in *Yellow Pages* or call your local plumber.

FENCES AND GATES

Check with your house deeds whether a garden fence is your responsibility or that of your neighbour (see **Neighbours** section). Prevention of wear and tear is always better than replacement.

- Inspect regularly for loose posts or sections and screw or nail them into position.
- Apply wood preservative once a year, at a time when least damage will be done to climbing plants.
- Check that gateposts are standing firm. Re-inforce with angle brackets if necessary (having first removed the gate).
- If screws have rusted, remove them (using a lubricant or blowtorch) and replace, plugging the holes if necessary.
- Replace hinges as necessary.
- Apply wood preservative to wooden gates regularly.
- Remove all rust and corrosion from metal gates so that you expose the bare metal. Apply zinc primer below the top coat.

GUTTERS

Cleaning   Avoid ineffective gutters and blocked drainpipes by clearing them once a year to remove leaves and other debris. Use a trowel and a wire brush and take care not to push or lose anything down the drainpipe. If you are cleaning a lot of debris, plug the downpipe with an old rag while you're doing the job and take a bucket with you to collect rubbish – don't just drop it on to the ground.

Repairs
- While you are up there, check the joints. In metal guttering, these may have corroded and leaked.
- Minor leaks can sometimes be cured with two or three applications of heavy-grade bituminous paint on the inside. If not, you will have to remove whatever is holding the sections together and clean out the joint. Treat with a rust inhibitor

and repack with mastic. Replace or renew the fittings.

- Joints in plastic gutters can sometimes be pushed into position or resealed with a jointing clip and seal. If your gutters collect a lot of debris, you can fit a mesh grid over the top to prevent them from becoming clogged. But you will still have to ascend from time to time to check the mesh..

- Cracking along the length of the gutter is usually caused by frost. Clean the gutter well and use impregnated waterproof tape to repair the crack, making sure it is firmly stuck down.

- Check the screws and brackets fixing the gutter to the fascia board and replace if necessary.

- To clear a clogged downpipe, first cover the drain at the bottom so that if you push the blockage down it doesn't subsequently block the drain. Ideally, try to pull the blockage out at the top of the drain using either a piece of wire with a hook bent at the end or a specialist tool (available from hire shops). Flush the pipe using a garden hose to clear remaining debris. Prevent a recurrence by capping the downpipe with garden netting or a purpose-designed wire cage.

- Minor cracks in downpipes can be repaired (while you wait to replace them) by using either self-adhesive flashing tape or epoxy repair paste and glass-fibre bandaging.

PATHS AND PATIOS

Clean these as **Steps** (see over) if growth has built up. Otherwise, sweep regularly and remove weeds growing in cracks with a proprietary weed killer.

Broken Replace broken paving stones carefully. *Paving stones* Wear protective goggles and gloves and lever out the broken stone using a hammer and cold chisel to cut outwards from the centre. Clean out the recessed area and put in a layer of sand or ready-mix cement. Insert the new slab, making sure it is firmly embedded and level with the surrounding ones. Fill the gaps with mortar and brush clean.

Uneven   Level an uneven paving stone by levering it out, putting in sand or ready-mix cement and repositioning until level.

ROOFS

Faulty flashings   These can be repaired with self-adhesive flashing tape. Remove the damaged flashing and clear the surrounding area. Apply flashing primer followed by the appropriate width of tape. Press it firmly into position with the end of a broom handle.

If you are not confident of your ability to work on a roof, employ professional help.

Flat roofs   They don't last for ever but if damage is not too bad they can be patched up temporarily. If damp has got into the home it is sensible to replace the flat roof, as sealing in water can produce rot.

Blisters   Should be cut with a sharp knife into a cross formation. Clean the exposed area, fill with bituminous mastic and press the edges down firmly. Cover with a further layer of mastic.

Cracks   Should be cleaned out (use a portable car vacuum cleaner if necessary) and filled with bituminous mastic. Cover with glass-fibre bandage and apply a further layer of mastic or use a roof repair kit (from d-i-y stores).

Shed roofs

They are usually small enough to make refelting a d-i-y job when it becomes necessary. Pull out the roofing nails and remove the old felt. Clean the boards and apply a coat of wood preservative. Buy new felt (the heavier grades are better) and a bitumen-based adhesive. Lay the felt in strips, starting at the bottom edge of the roof and allowing enough to cover the eaves. Fix with clout nails (a nail with a large flat head) all round. Apply adhesive to the top edge and stick the next strip down over it. Nail into position. At the corners, and wherever there is a ridge, make a neat fold and nail firmly.

Slates and tiles

Loose or fallen tiles and slates should be put back or replaced. If this is not straightforward, call in a roofing contractor but do not be swayed by an argument that you need a completely new roof unless you believe this to be true. Get a second or third opinion if necessary.

STEPS

Outside steps can be victim to a build-up of algae and moss to the point where they become slippery as well as unattractive.

- Treat the beginnings of a problem with a solution of household bleach (60ml of household bleach to 5 litres of water) applied with a stiff brush, left for ten minutes, then rinsed off with clean water.
- Where algae and moss have a firm grip, apply a special patio cleaner (from garden centres and d-i-y stores) and wear old clothes, protective boots and gloves.
- If cracks appear once growth has gone, use an exterior filler to repair them.

WALLS

Repointing
- Use a hammer and cold chisel to remove crumbling mortar from between bricks but don't gouge out any that is sound or the bricks may become loose. With a paintbrush or hand-held vacuum cleaner, get rid of the dust.
- Dip a paintbrush in water and wet the joints you are going to repoint to prevent the brickwork from absorbing water from the new mortar, thus preventing it from sticking firmly.
- Mix the new mortar, taking care not to make it too sloppy or too dry. Mix only in small quantities or it will dry out before you use it.
- Place some plastic sheeting along the base of the wall to catch any mortar that you drop. If you are quick it can be re-used.
- Put some mortar on a hawk (a small hand-held board) and with a pointed trowel press it firmly between the bricks and along the length of the joint. Do vertical joints first, then horizontal, working on an area of about a square metre at a time.
- Match the finish of your repointing to that already on the brickwork.

POINTING

- *Flush pointing*   This is the easiest to do and is level with the face of the bricks.

- *Recessed pointing*   It is created by smoothing off the mortar with a round-headed rod.

- *Weatherstruck joints*   These are recessed at the top to help rainwater run off the brickwork.

WINDOWS

- Wear thick protective gloves and goggles while removing all the broken glass from the window frame.

- Use a small hammer to tap until the pieces are loose. Wrap the pieces of broken glass in several layers of old newspaper before putting them in the refuse bin or taking them to the local tip. If you are replacing an upstairs pane, put an old blanket down to catch any pieces that fall and ensure that no one is walking underneath while you are working.

- Chip out the old putty from the rebates (the channels in which the glass sits) using a wood chisel. Pull out any fixings and, if they look reusable, save them, especially the small clips used on metal frames. With wooden frames, take the opportunity to check the timber for rot and treat if necessary.

- Measure the frame carefully. You need a piece of glass which is 3mm less than the height *and* width of the frame to allow for the rebates. Check the diagonals to see if the frame is truly square (or rectangular); if not, allow for this in the measurements. If you are not happy taking measurements yourself, call in a glazier. Have the glass cut to size professionally.

- Mix or buy ready-mixed putty and spread a bed of it along all the rebates. Put the glass in position and press evenly around the edges until it is correctly positioned. Do not press in the centre or you may break the pane. Squeeze out as much putty as possible and scrape it away with a putty knife moistened in water to give a good finish. Finish it off at an angle to allow for rain to run off. Leave to dry for at least a week before repainting.

Broken panes

Frames   *Rotting*   Cut out the rotten area, going a couple of inches at least into the good wood on either side. Treat the bare surfaces with wood preservative and glue in a new piece of wood – also treated with wood preservative on all sides. To prevent rot from appearing, check all frames every year and repaint regularly.

Rusting   Treat as soon as it appears since the frames will have to be replaced if rust gets a hold. Wear protective goggles and gloves and remove as much as possible with steel wool or a wire brush. Clean the exposed surface with a rust remover, wash, dry and apply metal primer and a top coat of paint.

Jammed windows   These usually result from being clogged with paint. Use a paint stripper to remove the paint from the jammed point, rub down, prime and repaint. Do not close the window until the paint is thoroughly dry.

Sash cords   These need replacing when they become worn, although you can make them last longer by rubbing them occasionally with a cake of soap or a candle to keep them running smoothly.

- Enlist a helper when you replace a cord. Even small windows are heavy and you will not be able to manage alone.
- In a lower window, first lever off the beading strips with a chisel. Try not to break them or you will have to buy new ones. Lift the window a few inches and pull it forward, i.e. away from the frame. Rest the side with the broken cord on a piece of furniture, getting your helper to hold it steady, and remove the strip of timber covering the weight compartment at the bottom of the frame. Take out the weight.
- Pull out the broken cord and use the pieces to measure the exact length of new cord. Fix one end of the new cord to the weight.
- Take a piece of weighting material – a length of chain or a curtain weight – and tie it to a piece of string. Put the weighted end into the casing over

the pulley and feed it down till you see it. Fix the loose end of the string to prevent it from slipping down the casing, remove the weight from the other end and tie the string to the non-weighted end of the sash cord. Pull it up and over the top of the pulley and fix the weighted end back in position.

- Get your helper to lift the window close to the frame and secure the cord in the same way as previously. Move the window gently up and down to check that the cord is the right length, then put it into position and replace the wood over the weight and the beading strips.

- Replace a sash cord on a top window in the same way, but first remove the lower sash from its frame so that you can remove the parting beading between the two frames. You can then swing the top sash out but will need something like a cupboard or ladder on which to rest it.

Cycles and cars

• Cycles   • Cars

Keep home transport well maintained, having it serviced professionally when necessary, so that it won't let you down.

CYCLES

General maintenance   Clean your cycle and lightly oil the chain, gear changers and cogs regularly. If you over-oil, this will collect dirt and grit causing wear – grit should be cleaned off before oiling.
Carry the following items in your basic tool kit:
- spare inner tube
- tyre levers (three)
- spare tyre valve (if removable)
- all-purpose adjustable spanner or dumb-bell spanner and/or Allen keys
- screwdriver (flat blade and Phillips)
- long-nosed pliers
- batteries and bulbs for lamps
- garden wire for make-shift repairs
- basic first-aid kit (see **Accidents at home** section)

Valves   • When a tyre goes flat slowly, first check the valve. Turn the wheel until the valve is at the top. Remove the cap, re-inflate the tyre and put the valve in a bowl of water. If bubbles appear, the valve is faulty and should be replaced. If there are no bubbles, you'll need to check for a puncture.

There are two main types of valve.

Schroeder Just screw on the bicycle pump connector and inflate. Mainly found on mountain bikes.

Presta Has a knurled knob on top that needs unscrewing before you can pump it up (the knob unscrews a few turns, then stops, i.e. it shouldn't be fully removed). After inflating the tube, screw the knob back up.

Punctures

- Turn the bike to stand on the saddle and handlebars. It is often easier to remove the wheel at this point. Loosen the nuts or open the quick-release mechanism. If it is a back wheel of a cycle with derailleur gears, putting it into top gear (the smallest of the cogs) before removing the wheel will make it easier. Unscrew any nut which holds the valve assembly and lever off the tyre using tyre levers and then your fingers. Spoon handles can be substituted for tyre levers.
- Pull out the inner tube and partly inflate it using the bicycle pump. Carefully run your fingers around the inner tube until you come to the puncture – indicated by air coming out. Put your ear to the tube and you will be able to hear air escaping; alternatively, run the inner tube through water till you find the puncture, then dry the inner tube. Mark the spot with the crayon supplied in the puncture repair kit.
- Clean the surface of the inner tube with the glasspaper provided, to give an area to stick the patch to. Apply rubber solution and wait for it to become tacky.
- Fit a patch from the repair kit and sprinkle talcum powder or French chalk over the repair to stop the inner tube sticking to the inside of the tyre.
- Check the inside of the tyre, in case what caused the puncture is still present.
- Push the valve through the rim of the wheel, fit the locknut (not too tight at this stage) and replace the valve core – if the removable type.
- Partly inflate the tube and roll it under the edge

of the tyre and over the rim of the wheel. Press the tyre into position on the wheel.

- Taking care not to nip the inner tube, push the valve into the rim and tighten the valve locknut. (If it is the back wheel, wrap the chain around the sprocket before slotting the axle into the forks.) Inflate the tyre.

If you puncture away from home, it is far simpler to carry a spare inner tube and fit that than spend time mending a puncture on the open road.

Brakes   Warning signs of dodgy breaks are squeaking and juddering, a slack feeling when you pull them and the need to move the brake lever more than halfway for the brake to function effectively.

[A juddering front brake can also indicate a loose headset. The headset is the housing containing ball bearings and is located at the top of the front forks. It enables the cyclist to turn the front wheel freely. If you suspect that it is the headset that is causing the problem, take the cycle to a cycle shop for repair.]

Nowadays there are two types of brakes.

Side-pull and centre-pull (road and racing cycles and some mountain bikes).

Cantilever (most mountain bikes and some good touring cycles).

- Loosen the locknut on the adjusting barrel (often found on the brake itself for side-pull, or brake lever for cantilever) and screw the barrel away from the nut. Check the correct position and screw up the locknut.
- If the adjusting barrel is already as far away from the locknut as possible, screw it right in, then unscrew the anchor bolt and tighten the brake cable at the caliper. Do up the anchor bolt. For cantilever brakes you may need to re-centralise the brakes after doing this.

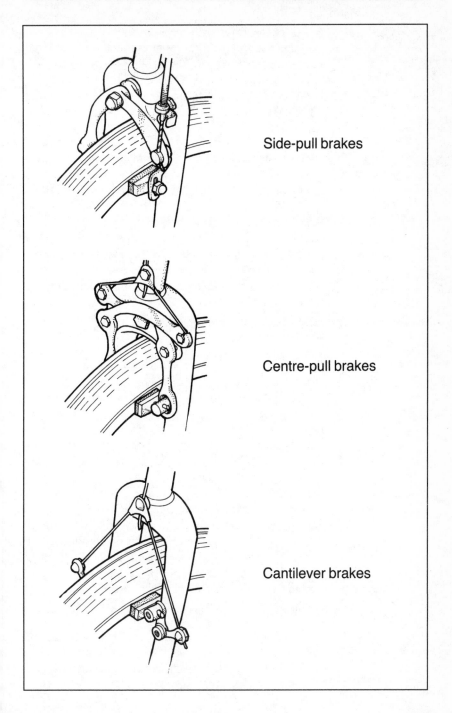

Side-pull brakes

Centre-pull brakes

Cantilever brakes

- To check that the brakes are now working correctly, push the cycle along at a walking pace and apply both brakes. The wheels should be immobilised immediately.

Brake blocks Braking can be a problem if brake blocks are worn or if they are not hitting the wheel rim squarely.

You can buy new brake blocks for side-pull and centre-pull brakes and fit them into the existing brake shoes; for cantilever brakes the blocks are almost invariably moulded on to the shoes and have to be bought as a unit.

Brake cables If a cable becomes frayed and worn you will need to replace it. Be sure to check where the cable enters the brake lever as this is a common place for fraying, yet is often hidden. To remove a cable, loosen the cable anchor bolt and pull out the cable. You may also need a new outer cable. Grease the inner cable first, and it will slide into the outer cable more easily.

Gears   *Derailleur* Re-tighten the central bolts on the control levers every so often to prevent the gears slipping. Adjust the tension of the cable by pulling it taut through the cable anchor bolt on the changer; re-set the adjustable stopscrews on the changer so that it moves easily into top and bottom gears. Indexed gears need special adjustment – refer to the cycle's set of instructions.

Three-speed hub If the gears are slipping, put the gear control into middle gear. Undo the locknuts beneath the cable connector, while looking through the window-hole in the extension of the wheel nut until you see that the end of the indicator rod, which is joined on to the short length of chain, comes exactly level with the end of the axle. Simply re-tighten the locknut.

What size cycle?   You can work out the frame size you require by following the calculations below. For a standard cycle, take your inside leg measurement and deduct nine inches – that is your frame size. (Another way of doing the calculation is to divide your height in inches by three.) Cycle frame sizes generally increase in ½ inch increments. For a mountain bike, do the same inside leg measurement calculation but deduct an *extra* two to four inches from your result.

Minor changes to fit a rider can be made by altering the saddle and handlebar heights (see below).

Saddle height Move a pedal to its lowest position; you should be able to sit comfortably on the saddle with the ball of your foot upon the pedal. Your knee will be slightly stretched. For safety you should be able to touch the floor with the toes of both feet.

Handlebar height The handlebars should be at the same height as the saddle or slightly higher. The distance from the point of the saddle to the centre of the handlebars should correspond to the distance from your elbow to the tips of the fingers.

Security

- Get your cycle frame marked with your postcode. The local cycle shop or police station may do this free of charge.
- Keep a note of the serial number of your cycle (often to be found under the pedal housing) as well as the colour, make and model. Take a photograph of the cycle.
- Buy a U-shaped cycle lock and use it. Some come with a year's cycle insurance. When leaving a cycle locked up, remember to pass the lock through the frame *and* the wheels to prevent these from being stolen. With quick-release wheels you should release the front wheel and lock it alongside the rear wheel.
- Take all accessories, i.e. pump, panniers, with you when you leave the cycle – you may also want to remove the saddle (if fitted with a quick-release bolt), which is easy for a thief to steal and renders the cycle almost unridable should the thief have persevered and broken through your security system.
- In some instances you cannot get your household insurance policy to cover a bicycle; it needs to be insured independently (see **Insurance** section).

Train travel   Bicycles generally travel free on British Rail, but there are many and varied exceptions to this rule, depending upon the route taken, the time of day, the day of the week and the type of rolling stock. On certain trains you also have to book in advance. Full details are in *The Rail Traveller's Guide to Biking by Train* which is available from stations. Bicycles travel in the guard's van (where the train has one) and should not be locked to fixtures as the guard may sometimes need to move the cycles during the course of the journey. They should also be labelled with your name and address.

Personal cycle insurance   Third party accident insurance is automatically available by joining the Cyclists' Touring Club (annual membership £24). Details from Cyclists' Touring Club (CTC) (see **Addresses**).

CARS

General maintenance
- Check oil, radiator and screen washer levels each week.
- Check that all lights work, especially in winter. Carry spare bulbs.
- In the winter, regularly hose under the wings to remove mud or salt deposits.
- Check tyres for stones or nails in the tread and for cuts in the sidewalls.
- Carry a spare can of fuel if you're going on a long journey.

It is illegal to drive a car if its horn, lights or windscreen wipers do not work.

Faulty horn   The most likely reason is a blown fuse.
- Find the fuse box by checking the car handbook.
- Where you have a system of numbered fuses, the handbook will tell you which one affects the horn.

- Replace with a new fuse of the same rating. If this immediately blows, go to a garage and have the wiring repaired.

Headlights Open the bonnet and locate the back of the headlight unit. Pull the electric wiring free. If the new bulb is of the quartz halogen type, take care not to touch the bulb with your fingers. Use a cloth instead. Place the new bulb in position and reconnect the wiring.

Tail and brake lights See *Headlights* above – access in this case may be via the boot or from the outside.

Faulty lights

Wiper arms
- Set the wipers into their normal position, noting where the blade rests on the screen. Fit the blade to the new arm (see below) and remove the old wiper arm. You will probably find a screw or clip beneath the cover at the base of the wiper arm.
- Position the new arm and blade on the spindle and return the arm to its normal position. Fasten by replacing the screw or clip into position.

Wiper blades
- Simply buy the appropriate blades and reverse the removal procedure for re-inserting.

Windscreen wipers

- Remove the hub cap, and then loosen, by half a turn only, each nut on the wheel you want to remove with a wheelbrace.
- Put the jack in place (check your car's handbook for the precise position) and raise the car until the wheel is clear of the ground.
- Remove the wheel nuts completely, then lift off the tyre and wheel and place the spare wheel in its place.
- Lightly tighten the wheel nuts, then lower the jack and remove.
- Finally, tighten the nuts fully, working in sequence on diagonal pairs to ensure that the wheel is centralised.

Changing a wheel

Flat battery   *Jump start*   Requires the use of a car with a charged-up battery.

- Park the car with the working battery near the car with the flat battery – not against it.
- Join the jump leads to the correct terminals on both batteries: positive to positive, negative to negative. Don't let the leads touch the sides of the cars.
- Run the engine on the working car, then try the starter on the disabled car. Run for ten seconds with breaks of thirty seconds in between (this should work within three or four attempts).
- Disconnect the jump leads by removing one lead entirely before the other.

Push start   Not possible on a car with an automatic gearbox.

- If possible, a car should be push started facing downhill.
- Turn the ignition on and depress the clutch; have the gear lever in second gear.
- When the pusher/s have picked up momentum the driver should lift his/her foot sharply from the clutch. If the engine fires, the driver should keep it revving while depressing the clutch again.

Dirty windscreens   See **Windows** in **Household and cleaning problems** section.

Keys locked inside car
- Consider keeping a spare key hidden somewhere on the car, fixed by a magnet to the inside of the wing or taped behind the bumper. Otherwise, call the police, a motoring organisation or a garage, all of whom should be able to get in easily.

Frozen car lock   If you don't have a can of de-icer, the following may work.
- Heat the car key using a lit match or a cigarette lighter. Leave the warmed key in the lock for a few seconds, to give it a chance to thaw the lock, before turning it. Don't apply pressure or the key may break.

- Reduce the chances of icing-up by covering the key holes with masking tape when the car is being washed. Also, oil the locks regularly with thin penetrating oil.

- If the door won't open, even when unlocked, move the handle up and down a few times in order to free it. **Frozen door lock**
- If this fails, spray de-icer between the door and the door pillar at a point just above the latch.

- Mark car windows with the registration number. **Security**
- Fit a Krooklok or similar device that locks the steering wheel, or hand brake and gear lever in place.
- Get a car alarm fitted. Newer versions of car alarms tend not to go off when the car is merely leant against, but actually require someone to enter the car before the alarm is set off.
- Get an engine immobiliser fitted.
- Install a removable or coded radio/tape/CD-player.
- Hide your valuables out of sight, but preferably don't leave them in the car at all.
- Park in a well-lit and busy place.

Neighbours

- Noisy neighbours
- Parking problems
- Garden problems
- Other problems

It is in the interest of everyone for neighbours to develop a reasonable relationship with each other and to be able to discuss any problems that arise as a result of close proximity. Always try to discuss a problem before taking Draconian steps which can only worsen a relationship.

In urban areas, there are likely to be people other than yourself who are irritated by a particular neighbourhood problem. Complaints will be more effective if you can get together to make them. Consider involving the local Residents' or Tenants' Associations if this is the case.

NOISY NEIGHBOURS

Excessive noisiness is hard to define but is one of the main causes of friction between neighbours. While there is little you can do about a persistently crying baby or an occasional piece of d-i-y, there is action you can take over regular noise if you can prove that it interferes with your enjoyment of your home, and so amounts to a nuisance.

Burglar and car alarms These should, if correctly installed, cease ringing after a specific period of time. Call the police if the noise continues, especially if the alarm is in a commercial building.

Unless someone is running a business that uses power tools in the home, you can take heart from the fact that, eventually, all d-i-y projects come to an end. Try to persuade your neighbour to carry out work only during the day.

D-i-y activity

If you're bothered by persistent dog barking, and talking to your neighbours doesn't help, put your complaint in writing to the dog's owner and keep a copy. Keep a diary of the dates and times when the barking has occurred. If possible, get other people who are affected to join in with your complaint.

Dog barking

Follow the same procedures as for **Dog barking** (see above).

Loud music/ TV

Where your neighbour insists that an instrument needs to be practised regularly, try to arrange a specific period during the day when the noise will irritate you least. You could also come to a similar agreement about lawn-mowing if this is done regularly at a time of day which disturbs you.

Musical instruments

Call the police if a noisy party goes on after midnight and you can't stand it or it's keeping small children awake. But try not to be a killjoy if it's just a one-off.

Parties

Ask the landlord to put up a notice requesting customers to be quiet when leaving the pub and not to slam car doors late at night.

Pub noise

In each of these cases, the final step should be to call in the Environmental Health Officer, who can get the council or magistrates' court to issue a noise abatement order which requires the offender to ensure that the noise stops. Alternatively, you can obtain a court injunction or launch your own prosecution.

Final courses of action

GARDEN PROBLEMS

Bonfires Try to reach an agreement with your neighbour on a suitable time of day for a bonfire. If your neighbour has them frequently you can ask the local authority to take action.

Fence in disrepair If a garden fence is in a state of disrepair, first check the deeds of your home to see if you own the fence. If not, you will have to persuade your neighbours to repair it. You can claim compensation only if the damaged fence causes you financial loss. This is hard to prove where flowers and shrubs are being affected but should be possible if, for example, your neighbour's fence damaged a greenhouse. For the sake of your own property's appearance it might be worth offering to pay half the cost of repair or replacement (see also **Fences and gates** in **External problems** section).

Trees *Branches* If your neighbours' tree branches are hanging over your property, you can cut them off at the point where they come over your fence or wall but you must return the branches and any fruit on them to your neighbours. It's wise to warn your neighbours that you're going to do this as they may prefer to prune the tree themselves.

Roots If tree roots from next door are affecting your home's foundations, check your household insurance policy; you should be able to claim on it. If the roots are coming in from 'public' trees in the road, you can claim either against the local authority or, in the case of a trunk road, the Department of Transport. You are entitled to cut roots which are protruding into your garden.

PARKING PROBLEMS

Can't park outside your home?

Alas, you have no right to park outside your own home. Introducing residents' parking may solve parking problems in a crowded area (the Residents' or Tenants' Associations can press for this), but this in turn can create problems for daytime visitors.

Caravans in drives

This may spoil the appearance of the area, but there's nothing you can do about it.

Entrance to your home blocked

If people persistently park across the entrance to your home, call the police to ask if they'll tow the vehicles away.

Parking on grass verges

Ask the local authority to intervene on your behalf.

In general, parking regulations state that you must not park on pavements and you must not block a road because this could prevent access by the emergency services.

OTHER PROBLEMS

Derelict house

If a house in your road is derelict, with its garden overgrown, the local authority can take action under the Public Health Act and either get the owner to tidy the place up or do it itself and bill him or her.

Development in the area

Keep a close eye on planning applications, which should be posted on any building that is going to be altered. Make your objections known, if you have any. If a neighbour is planning an extension which will affect your home, talk to the planning department of your local authority.

163

Dry/wet rot   If your neighbour's dry/wet rot is coming through the wall and damaging your property, your neighbour should rectify the damage. You may be entitled to claim compensation.

Horses   If horses from the local riding school leave mess all over the road, you can ask the local authority to clear it up.

Litter   It is an offence to leave litter in open-air spaces, so if there is litter from, for example, a fast-food outlet all over the road to which the public has access, get the local authority to provide more litter bins and, if necessary, prosecute offenders.

5

A LITTLE EXTRA HELP

Moving house
Hiring help
Insurance
Holidays

Moving house

- Removal firms   • Specialist removals
- Advance planning   • Change of address
- Do as you would be done by   • Miscellaneous

Most of the problems which can arise whilst moving house occur because of a lack of planning – at both ends of the move. Even if time is a problem *make* time to get your old and new homes sorted out. Otherwise, you'll *need* time to untangle the chaos which is likely to result.

REMOVAL FIRMS

Finding a company

To find a good removal company, look in *Yellow Pages* under 'Removals and storage' and phone the British Association of Removers (see **Addresses**) to ask for the names of members in your area. Friends may also be able to recommend removal firms they have used to their satisfaction.

Getting an estimate

- Get a minimum of three estimates, each of which will require a visit by an estimator to your home. (If you're moving only a small amount of stuff – perhaps from a studio flat – ask if you can be a part-load on someone else's major removal.) Check that the estimates include VAT and decide on the firm you want.
- Show the estimator *everything* that is to be moved. This includes things that might slip your mind, such as fitted carpets and shelving systems, and things that need special attention,

for example, a grand piano (see page 169) or expensive fine wines.

- When you've accepted an estimate, finalise the details. The removers should be aware of any access problems (getting large wardrobes up or down narrow stairs) and should sort out parking availability with the police at both places.

Insurance

Sort out the insurance, including a goods-in-transit policy (particularly if transit involves an overnight stop). You can insure through the removers or through your normal household insurers. Check the details thoroughly. Most removal policies require you to check goods within a few days of arrival. Failure to do this (or to make an arrangement for delay) may mean you can't claim.

Packing your possessions

Be wary of agreeing to pack your own possessions. If the removers do the packing and items then get damaged, you can claim on your insurance. If you pack, there may be problems. Check that any savings made by doing the packing yourself are worthwhile overall.

D-I-Y REMOVALS

A d-i-y move is worth doing only if:

- you don't have a lot of stuff

- you can drive (or know someone who can) a van big enough to move things within a reasonable period of time and without too many trips. Note that for vans over 7.5 tons you need an HGV licence

- you and whoever is helping you can lift and manoeuvre any heavy items you own

- paying for petrol, overnight stops, meals and so on for helpers won't cost as much as hiring professionals.

SPECIALIST REMOVALS

Electrical equipment Hi-fi equipment, video recorders and computers or word processors should ideally be moved in special boxes supplied by the removal firm or in the boxes in which they were bought. Since you've probably thrown these away, ask your local dealers if they can supply you with something suitable.

Grandfather clocks These need to be dismantled and put together at the other end by an expert. Your removal firm may be able to put you in touch with one; otherwise, consult a local specialist clock shop or antique dealer.

Houseplants Take them with you rather than putting them in the removal van. Wedge them into tea chests or strong boxes, using crumpled newspaper to keep them in place, cover the top with polythene or cling film to minimise temperature variations.

Large household appliances Large household appliances, such as cookers, dishwashers and washing-machines, usually have instructions for moving in their handbooks. If not (or if you've lost them), consult your electricity or gas service centre or refer to the original supplier or the manufacturer.

Pets Pets may not travel in a removal van, so you must arrange for their transport. It may be sensible to put cats and dogs into boarding kennels for a few days so that they are not disturbed by the upheaval. Tortoises should be boxed up safely. Small caged animals and birds can travel in their cages. Birds should have a cloth over the top to encourage them to rest rather than beat against the bars. Cold-water fish, such as goldfish, should travel in large plastic bags (containing 25 per cent water and 75 per cent air) suspended in a bucket. Tropical fish need special care; consult your local specialist shop.

Pianos, especially valuable ones, should be moved by a specialist company. This may be the remover you are employing or you may need to use another firm with skilled staff and the right equipment. Allow a piano time to recover from its journey before having it retuned.

Pianos

Refrigerators and freezers should be emptied. Wash the insides with a solution of bicarbonate of soda (30ml bicarbonate of soda to 2 litres warm water). Dry thoroughly. Put a charcoal-based 'no smell' fridge product inside each appliance to prevent odours building up while the doors are closed during removals.

Refrigerators

ADVANCE PLANNING

In a perfect world, you should have anything that needs doing to your home done *before* you move in. If there *is* some time available, consider whether you can get any of the following done – if necessary. Ask the current occupants of your new home to recommend firms.

This may need installing or upgrading. Get several estimates.

Central heating

Have chimneys swept if they need it.

Chimneys

You may need a complete damp course or merely need to treat mildly damp areas appropriately. If condensation is causing damp, work out how to improve ventilation.

Damp treatment

Your solicitor should have a written document listing the fittings (appliances, floorcoverings, curtains etc.) that are to be left for your use. If the home is going to be bare, you may want to measure up and have some floorcoverings and curtains/blinds ordered and fitted before you move.

Fittings

STORAGE

If you have to store furniture because of a delay between moving out and moving in:

- get a quotation for the weekly/monthly cost
- check that your goods are covered by insurance against loss, theft, fire, flood and damage
- have carpets and furnishings cleaned and mothproofed before storing
- put moth repellent in with any clothes that are stored.

Redecoration If you're buying a wreck, having a couple of rooms done up (professionally or by yourself) will raise morale. Depending on your lifestyle, prime sites will probably be your own or your children's bedrooms, kitchen, bathroom and a living room.

Reroofing/ Complete reroofing is best done in summer, so if
replacing tiles you're making a winter move, you may have to live with leaks for a season.

Rewiring Your surveyor should have told you if this is necessary. Even if basic wiring is in good order, you may want to add new socket outlets or double existing ones.

Woodworm If woodworm treatment is required, it would be
treatment preferable to have it done before you move in, even if it means leaving a gap before moving.

What goes Think about where major items of furniture are to
where? go in your new home. You don't want to be shifting heavy pieces around yourself. You may like to draw up floor plans showing where specific items are to be situated.

Devise a system of colour coding. Put the same colour sticker on all items that are to go in a particular room and stick the same colour on its door when you arrive so that the removers know where to put things. Try to get stickers which will come off again easily, to avoid damaging the furniture.

CHANGE OF ADDRESS

You'll need to tell all sorts of people about your move and also make arrangements for having meters, such as electricity meters, read. You should also ensure that the person whose house you are buying has had the meters read so that you don't end up paying a bill that isn't your own. Use the following list to remind you what needs doing and tick off items as you do them. If you make any arrangements on the telephone, confirm them in writing and keep a copy.

Banks

Give your new address to all banks with which you have accounts. If you want to move your account to your new location, make arrangements with the managers. After you've moved, check that your new bank has full details of any standing orders and direct debits. If you keep an item in a bank safe-deposit, make secure arrangements for moving it to a new location.

Cars

Inform the Driver Vehicle Licensing Centre (see **Addresses**) of your move. Include details of your car's registration number and make. Also, make sure you have the address on your driving licence changed.

Charities

Send your new address to those charities with which you are in regular correspondence through donations or gift buying.

Council tax   Inform the appropriate department of the local authority in both areas.

Credit cards   Send your new address to the address on your statement, giving your account number.

Doctor/dentist   If you need to, ask your doctor/dentist to recommend someone in your new area. Otherwise, wait until you arrive and see if you can obtain a personal recommendation or get a list of local doctors/dentists from the public library.

Dry-cleaning   Collect outstanding items (the same goes for shoes being repaired).

Electricity company   Ask for a meter reading on moving day. Inform the electricity company of your new address and, if moving into a new area, sign on with the new company. Avoid having electricity disconnected and having to pay a reconnection charge. Check that the people moving out of your new home have arranged to have the meter read that day.

Employer   Provide your new address and, if necessary, details of your new bank account.

Family benefits   Check with the DSS or post office, or check in your benefit book for full details.

Football pools   Put your new address on the coupon or personally give it to your collector.

Gas   (See **Electricity** above.)

Giro   Ask at the post office about procedures.

Hire purchase   Give your address to companies with whom you have an agreement.

Hospital   Give your new address to your hospital, clinic or day centre and, if necessary, arrange (through your GP) for a transfer.

If you are self-employed, send your new details to the address on your tax form. If employed, your employer will do this. Ask your personnel department to confirm in writing that it's been done. *Income tax*

Send your new address to your insurers – in good time in case the move affects cover. *Insurance*

Settle accounts and cancel delivery of milk and papers. *Local traders*

Get a form from the post office to arrange for mail to be forwarded for a convenient period of time. One fee covers all members of a household with the same surname. Send your new address to the Mailing Preference Service (see **Addresses**) if you wish to reduce the amount of junk mail sent to your new home. *Mail*

Send your new address. There is usually space for this on the statement you are sent. *Mail order*

As with income tax, your employer will do this for you if you are employed. *National Insurance*

Fill in your new address in the space provided in your deposit book. *National Savings*

Get form P80MA from the post office in your new area. Fill it in and the post office will arrange for your pension to be paid in the new location. *Pension*

Contact the Department of National Savings on (0253) 766151 for details. *Premium Bonds*

Remember to forward your new details. *Professional advisers*

Return books and tickets if you're moving to another borough. *Public library*

Schools   Make arrangements for leaving and starting as early as you can. Bear in mind that fee-paying schools will charge a term's fees if they don't get a term's notice.

Shops   If necessary, settle up and arrange to close accounts.

Standing orders   Inform any companies/individuals with whom you have a standing order or direct debit of your new address.

Stocks and shares   Send your new address to the company registrar – the address will be on your dividend slip. Also, inform your stockbroker.

Subscriptions   Send your new address to any clubs or magazines with which you have a subscription.

Telephone   Arrange to have your account charged up to removal day and to take over the line at your new home. If moving locally, check if you can take your existing number with you.

TV licence   Check your TV licence for details.

TV rental   Inform the company and make necessary arrangements.

VAT office   Send the VAT office your new address if you pay VAT.

Water company   Contact the water company to inform them of your new address. Check whether a refund is due.

DO AS YOU WOULD BE DONE BY

Amid the chaos of your own move, spare a thought for those coming into your home. Write out a list of details which may otherwise cause them time and trouble, for example, the location of the main stopcock (if not obvious), where the light switch is in a dark loft or a warning to keep an eye on a gutter which tends to get blocked. A list of local personnel and services is also handy, for example, newspaper delivery services, shoe repairer, cleaner and babysitter, as well as the doctor and dentist. Ask the owners of your new home if they will supply you with similar information.

In an ideal situation, it's a good idea to create a home logbook in which you record useful information about your home. It's an aid to you while you're living there and is something which will be of inestimable value to anyone taking over your home. The following are details you could put in it.

Home logbook

- Information on the history of your home and its previous owners (if known).
- Details of the structure – for example, when you had it rewired (with perhaps a wiring diagram), information about the central heating and plumbing systems etc.
- Information about decoration – for example, how much paint, wallpaper you used in each room, type of floorcovering etc., where you bought things that might need to be repaired or replaced.
- Details of any appliances, including handbooks, guarantees and the numbers to ring for servicing.
- Useful local information about taxis, take-aways, leisure facilities and other amenities.

You can buy special logbooks in which to record this kind of information, but these can be restrictive. Creating your own loose-leaf file with plastic pockets for things like instruction books allow you to log the information *you* need while living in your home, and enables you to extract that which you want to leave behind when moving. Kept in a handy place that everyone knows about, a home logbook becomes a household 'bible' for instant reference when home information of any kind is needed.

MISCELLANEOUS

Service charges If you are moving into a complex or block of flats where a service charge operates, find out or get your solicitor to find out when payments are due before you exchange contracts. In some complexes, residents have limited control over the way charges are fixed and the charges can be raised at the whim of the landlord and may not cover certain repairs or decorations. Be wary where this is the case and aim to pay a service charge which is controlled by the residents and covers specified and essential areas of maintenance and repair. Find out exactly what you are responsible for.

Credit problems If you have moved to an address where the previous occupants have had bad debts, you may find that you are unable to get credit because *their* debt is logged as being attached to *your* property (new legislation may change this).

You have the right to check what is listed at your new address and can arrange to have it changed.

Know your neighbourhood Joining a local residents' association is a good way of tuning in to the local life and also enables you to make your presence felt on issues on which you have strong views.

Residents' associations These can play an effective part in keeping an area the way its inhabitants want it to be by pressing for improvements to local facilities and amenities and preventing unwanted development.

Neighbourhood Watch   These groups are run in some areas by local people and police with the idea of keeping an eye out for local crime; many have been successful. If there is no group operating in the area, contact the Crime Prevention Officer at your local police station with a view to starting one.

MOVERS' SURVIVAL KIT

When you've done all this you still have to follow the van. Take with you the following:

- keys to your new home (if you have them already)
- bedding and towels
- clean clothes and appropriate shoes
- things to amuse the children
- some appropriate food and drink
- lavatory paper
- electric light bulbs, fuses and fuse wire
- plugs and adaptors
- self-sealing plug for sinks and basins
- first-aid kit
- basic tool kit (adjustable spanner, hammer, pliers and screwdriver)
- torch (with new or fully charged batteries)
- candles
- washing-up liquid and brush/cloth
- electric kettle
- vacuum flask
- can opener
- basic/disposable plates, cups, cutlery

- saucepan (and camping stove if there's no working cooker)
- notepad and writing implements
- address book, envelopes and stamps
- important documents, cash and jewellery which won't be covered by your removal insurance
- any regular medication
- spare spectacles
- cheque book, bank and credit cards
- driving licence, motor insurance document
- removal contract
- cash (some firms ask for cash on the day of removal).

Hiring help

- The right person   • The agreement
- Paying up   • Back-up systems
- If something goes wrong   • Hiring goods

Whether you want to hire help to do a one-off job, such as re-tiling the roof, or to work for you on a regular basis, such as looking after your children, you need to be sure that whoever you hire is:
- qualified for/capable of doing the job
- honest and reliable
- clear about what is involved
- happy about the remuneration you agree between you.

THE RIGHT PERSON

For child care you need to take special care to select the right person. You can, after all, write off to experience a broken ornament but you can not regard damage to children in the same light.

Child care and babysitting

For regular child care you have a choice of hiring a nanny, mother's help, child minder or au pair. For babies and pre-school children the best choice is a qualified nanny or child minder. For older children, mother's helps and au pairs provide unqualified care and supervision. They will live in your home and will also do some housework. Nannies may live in your home or come to you during the day (and may be shared with another family to cut costs). With child minders, your children go to their homes on a daily basis.

When interviewing for child care it is important to let candidates meet your children to see how they take to one another. It is also vital to be very specific about the duties involved and the way you want the children brought up. Outline duties, such as how far the walk to school is and how much shopping needs to be done.

Regular services

For a regular service, such as cleaning or gardening, local recommendation is an excellent source. Otherwise, use a local agency or place your own advertisement in a local paper or shop. Be specific about what is involved so that candidates are not misled. Don't describe as light housework acres of flooring which need a weekly scrub.

Technical, construction or decorating work

For technical, construction or decorating work around the home, local recommendation is again a good bet. Or, if you follow up a newspaper or newsagent's advertisement, ask the firm to give you the name of at least one satisfied customer and, if possible, check on the standard of work. Bear in mind that a decorator who has satisfactorily painted a small modern house may not be suitable for the fancy paint effects you require. For work that could damage the fabric of your home if not done properly – electrics, gas and plumbing – make sure that anyone you employ has a recognised qualification or is a member of a recognised body (see **Addresses** for details of trade associations).

THE AGREEMENT

Child care

With people employed to mind your children, it's a good idea to have a written contract which spells out duties, hours to be worked, pay and holidays. Even if this was made clear at interview stage the candidate may have forgotten, been for other interviews or be too shy or inexperienced to clarify matters. Spell out what you've agreed between you in the contract, including any restrictions on visits from friends during working hours or overnight.

With au pairs, whose English may be poor in the early days, write out duties as simply as possible and run through them. If the au pair's English is poor and communication is a problem, find a friend, neighbour, more experienced au pair or local language teacher to help with translation.

Babysitters also require careful selection. There is no legal minimum age for babysitters but it would be unwise to employ anyone who you do not feel could cope in an emergency. Babies may need changing and feeding while older children can produce discipline problems – and, of course, there is always the risk of fire or an accident. Always leave a telephone number where you can be reached, the number of your doctor and the number of a neighbour who can drive in cases of emergency.

In 1992, The British Red Cross introduced a training scheme for babysitters, offering advice on child care, first aid and what to do in an emergency. The scheme can be taught in schools or youth organisations. Ask would-be babysitters if they have taken part in it. Information on the scheme is available from The British Red Cross – see **Addresses**.

Domestic services

People hired to provide a regular domestic service do not usually require anything in writing stating their duties since these can usually be sorted out on an informal basis and altered when appropriate. However, if you are not going to be around when a new cleaner, for example, starts work, it might be helpful to write a list of the tasks you want done and where the tools and products are stored. It will probably save time in the long run if you can spend one or two sessions with a new employee explaining how you like things done.

Short-term contract work People hired to work on the fabric of your home will usually give you an estimate or quotation for the job. Check that it covers what you want done before agreeing to it and do not add in extra work without expecting to pay for it. A request from you to repoint the chimney while tiling the roof means extra labour, extra materials and extra cost to you. Think about that sort of thing in advance since it is difficult to exert cost control over work not included in the original estimate. Also agree on a contract covering when the work will begin and end, insurance, price, materials, who will clear up any rubbish and so on. Get everything in writing.

Common sense As an employer you have responsibilities to those who work for you beyond simply paying them.
Necessities Make sure that employees have whatever is necessary for them to do their jobs – petrol in the car's tank, a supply of cleaning products, for instance.
Time off Respect employees as human beings. They may from time to time be ill or have to attend a family funeral.
Be reasonable Avoid making employees feel envious if your material circumstances are better than theirs. Don't leave valuable items or credit cards around where they could get lost and give rise to suggestions of theft.

PAYING UP

Always agree in advance how you're going to pay people. For work on your home, a firm may well want some money up front to buy materials. Pay this but get a receipt for the money and insist on seeing the goods in case they've been ordered for someone else's job. For more complicated and longer work, the tradesperson may ask to be paid in instalments during the job as stages are completed. If you do agree to do this, write the stages into the contract. If you're not happy with the work done at any particular stage, then withhold payment at that stage until the work is done to your satisfaction (see **If something goes wrong** below). People such as cleaners and gardeners are usually self-employed, which means you pay them (usually in cash), but they are themselves responsible for declaring their earnings to the Inland Revenue.

Child carers may be self-employed (in which case *Child care* the above applies) or may require you, as part of the deal, to pay their income tax and National Insurance. Qualified nannies in particular tend to ask to receive a clear sum every week or month, so you need to allow for tax and insurance when calculating your outgoings. For details of how to pay, consult your local Inland Revenue office.

BACK-UP SYSTEMS

If you rely heavily on people who work regularly in your home, you will need a back-up network which can cope in cases of illness or holidays.

Agency staff, say for cleaning or gardening, will *Agency staff* probably cost more than you usually pay but should have been vetted by the agency.

A local network of friends and neighbours for child *Friends/* care should be set up *before* the need arises. *neighbours* Obviously, you have to be prepared to play your part, either personally or through your child carer.

183

INSURANCE

Check your contents and buildings insurance. You must be covered for any injury which might happen to an employee working in your home or on your garden, as well as for any damage which might be done to your property or possessions by the employee. Firms and individuals doing a specific piece of work on your home should have their own insurance which you should ask to check. You might find that a one-man-band decorator was not covered sufficiently when he sets fire to your home while blowtorching paint from your eaves.

IF SOMETHING GOES WRONG

Write immediately to the person you've hired, saying why you're not happy. If you've had no response after about seven days, send a recorded delivery letter outlining your problems again, warning that you will hire another tradesperson to complete the work if you hear nothing back within a specified time. Say that you will recover this expense from him/her.

Proof You will have to prove your claims. One way is to ask a new tradesperson to provide you with a fixed price for any work still needed and a report on the problems. It's also worth taking photographs of the substandard work. For larger jobs, it may well be worth getting an independent surveyor's report. But, if this doesn't resolve matters, the courts may be your only option.

Going to court Under the small claims procedure you can go to court without hiring a solicitor and can claim for the money it's cost to put the job right and for any specific losses (up to a maximum amount, which varies). For larger jobs, it is sensible to use a solicitor. It will cost more but may well prove worthwhile if you've lost a lot.

HIRING GOODS

Hiring is a good way of getting the use of goods which you use only infrequently and perhaps don't have room to store. If you shop around you'll find you can hire almost anything, but most domestic hiring is likely to concern specialist d-i-y equipment, items for parties and perhaps appliances such as washing-machines and televisions.

When hiring goods of any kind you should follow the following guidelines.

- Check what the total cost to you will be, including deposit, delivery and any extras you'll need.
- Check what the penalty will be if you over-run the hire period.
- Check the insurance in case you lose or damage the item you've hired.
- Check if you can return party equipment, such as crockery, cutlery and glasses, still dirty. You may have to pay a charge for this but it could save hours of washing-up. The hire agency will re-wash items when you return them anyway.
- Check arrangements for terminating a long-term hire agreement of appliances.
- Check what arrangements are made to cover appliances which go wrong. How quickly will they be repaired or replaced?

FIRMS WHICH HIRE OUT GOODS CAN BE FOUND IN THE *YELLOW PAGES* UNDER 'HIRE SERVICES'.

Insurance

- House insurance
- Car insurance
- Holiday insurance
- Complaints schemes

If you spill paint on your carpet, or if your golf clubs are stolen from your car, will your insurance company pay up? Check this chapter for a rough guide to what your insurance probably covers, and for tips to make sure your claim is successful.

HOUSE INSURANCE

House insurance comes in two parts – insurance for the buildings you live in, and insurance for the contents of your home. What's normally covered is listed below – but check your own policy to make sure it's not unusual.

Buildings   *What's covered?*   Your buildings insurance covers the building you live in and any outbuildings and underground pipes and cables connected to your building. This includes any permanent and immovable fixtures to the building, such as fitted bathrooms and kitchens. As well as covering the cost of any repair work, your buildings policy covers the cost of removing rubble and any necessary fees for architects, lawyers and surveyors.

Fences and gates are also covered under your buildings policy but there is no cover for damage by storms or floods. Swimming-pools and tennis courts are covered, but there is no cover for damage by subsidence or heave (see below).

What's covered? Your contents insurance covers all your possessions in your home which are portable, plus aerials and often, but not always, satellite dishes. Cover is available for the contents of your freezer but with some policies you have to pay extra for this. Items used for business purposes are not covered.

Contents

- All-risks insurance. Outside the home, your possessions will only be covered if you have taken out special all-risks insurance, available with your house contents policy. This will cover you against most eventualities, for example, if you accidentally leave your briefcase on the bus. This cover sometimes extends throughout the UK, sometimes throughout Europe and sometimes worldwide, so it can often be useful if you lose something on holiday. Cover for clothes outside the home is not usually available.
- In the garden. Cover for possessions in the garden will be limited to around £250 with most policies (but not all). Some policies only cover items 'temporarily removed' to the garden, not items which are permanently there, so if something is always in the garden, such as a swing or climbing frame, check to make sure it's covered. If it is permanently fixed to the ground, your buildings policy may cover it.
- Matching items. If you have matching items, e.g. a three-piece suite or carpets that match throughout the house, your insurance will pay to replace only the damaged items or only the carpet in the room where damage occurred. The insurers are obliged to pay any reasonable cost towards making or finding a matching replacement. However, if this is not possible they will still only pay to replace the damaged part, not the whole suite, or all the carpets. You can ask your insurance company to insure matching items as one item so that if any part is damaged all will be replaced, but this will cost extra.
- Moving house. If you are moving house, insurance companies will sometimes cover you for

any damage to your property in transit, so long as it is being moved by professional removers. If your policy does not cover this, you may find you can get insurance from the removal company (see **Moving house** section).

- Valuable items. If you have valuable items worth over a set amount (check your policy), these will only be covered if you have informed your insurers that you want them covered. Cover for stamp and coin collections is usually limited to around £500.

- Others. Money, securities, documents, cheque books and credit cards are covered in the home, usually up to a limit of around £200. Cover outside the home is also available, but you will probably have to pay extra.

  If your keys are stolen, most contents policies will pay for replacement locks for your house. Some policies will also pay for this if you simply lose your keys.

  Cycles, boats and caravans can all be covered under house contents insurance for an extra charge.

New for old   Most house contents insurance policies will pay to replace any damaged items with new ones – except for clothes, linen, pots and pans and, sometimes, cycles. You can buy 'indemnity insurance' which will only pay the actual value of whatever was damaged, but it may not be worth the saving in the long run. If, for example, you had a 10-year-old cooker damaged in a fire, your insurance would pay only for the value of a 10-year-old cooker only.

What you're   *Accidental damage* Your buildings policy will
covered   automatically cover you for accidental damage to
against   any fixed glass, ceramic hobs and washbasins, sinks, baths, toilets, shower trays, bidets etc. You will also be covered for accidental damage to underground pipes and cables.

Your contents policy will cover you for accidental damage to mirrors and plate glass in furniture. It will also cover you for accidental damage to hi-fis, TVs and videos – some policies exclude portable TVs while being carried. Some policies also automatically provide accidental damage cover for personal computers.

If you want to get accidental damage cover for anything else, you have to ask for an accidental damage cover extension, which will cost extra. But watch out for the exclusions:

- damage by pets
- accidental breakage of glass and fragile items
- accidental damage to valuables – e.g. jewellery, paintings, cameras
- spillage of wine or paint, say, on carpets.

These are sometimes covered as accidental damage and sometimes excluded, so if cover for any of these is important to you, make sure you buy a policy which provides it.

Legal liability   Your buildings insurance covers you for any legal liability as owner of your home. So, if a tile falls off the roof and hits someone on the head, you are covered. Your contents insurance covers you against personal legal liability. Or if you accidentally knock someone down, or if your dog tears the postman's trousers, you may find you can claim any costs you have to pay from your insurance.

Natural disasters and accidents   You are covered against damage by storms, floods, lightning, fire, earthquakes and explosions, and against damage by water or oil which escapes from your heating or plumbing system or from washing-machines and dishwashers (some policies also include fish tanks). You are also covered against damage by falling trees, branches and aerials; aircraft and objects falling from them; and collision by vehicles and animals. If your home is uninhabitable after a disaster, your insurance will pay some money towards alternative accommodation until you can move back.

Smoke, frost and freezing   Damage by smoke, frost and freezing is covered by some policies but not by others. So, if your pipes freeze and burst, *all* policies should cover you for the damage caused by the water escaping, but only *some* policies will also pay for the damage to the pipes.

Subsidence and heave This is when the land upon which your house is built rises or falls, which can cause cracks to appear in walls and, ultimately, makes your house unsafe to live in. House buildings and contents insurance provide cover against this but there are many exclusions. With most policies you will have to pay at least £500 towards the cost of any repairs. Also, it can take a lot of time and money to investigate the problem to discover whether damage to your house is really being caused by the ground moving. You will have to pay for this while you are making your claim. If you convince the insurance company that subsidence is causing the problem, they will pay for the investigation; otherwise you will have to pick up the bill.

Theft, vandalism, riots You are covered against any damage or loss caused by thieves, vandals and rioters. However, most policies do not cover you against theft by deception or fraud. Also, cover may be withdrawn or limited if you go away on holiday for a long time or if you rent out all or part of your home.

Wear and tear Storm damage is by far the most common cause of claims under buildings insurance. And the most common reason why these claims are not paid in full is wear and tear. If, say, a roof collapses in a storm, and you claim on your insurance, the insurers may argue that the roof collapsed partly because of the storm and partly because it was old and in poor condition and would have collapsed soon anyway. The insurance company will then make a deduction for wear and tear. Insurance companies often make a deduction for wear and tear on claims for damage to flat felt roofs, since they have a relatively short natural life. If your insurance company makes a deduction for wear and tear which you disagree with, try to get an expert (e.g. a builder or plumber) on your side to argue that the damage really was caused by the storm.

Some buildings policies guarantee not to make a deduction for wear and tear. However, you still have a duty to maintain your building in 'reasonable repair'. If you do not do this, your insurance company can refuse to pay your claim.

How much to insure for?

With some policies the premium depends on the number of bedrooms in your house; with others, on how much it would cost if everything insured was destroyed. With the latter, if you insure for too little, the company can refuse to pay the full amount.

Contents You have to insure for the cost of replacing all your possessions. Add up the cost of replacing everything in your home. The total figure is likely to astonish you, but it is the one you will have to pay a premium for. Don't forget to tell the insurance company every time you buy a new and reasonably expensive household item.

Buildings The amount for which you need to insure your building is based on how much it would cost to rebuild it. Advice on how to calculate what this would cost is available in a leaflet entitled *Building Insurance for Home-owners 1992* from the Association of British Insurers (see **Addresses**). Remember that this is the cost of rebuilding, not the likely resale value of your home.

You are legally obliged to tell your insurers of anything which might affect the risk they are taking on. In particular, you should tell your insurers if you have any lodgers, if you go away for a long holiday (more than 30 days), or if you are carrying out building/decorating work. Insurers often limit cover for theft, flood or accidental damage in these circumstances, but not always.

> ### MONEY-SAVING TIPS
>
> - You could get a discount on the cost of a policy by agreeing to pay a certain amount, a voluntary excess, towards any claim (for example, £50), with the insurance covering the remainder of the claim.
>
> - Many insurers offer discounts on house and car insurance if you fit extra security devices, such as locks or alarms, to your home or car.

Making your claim

The following tips should help your claim go as smoothly as possible.

- Make sure you have copies of any guarantees and receipts for new building work, or surveyors reports on your buildings.
- If there is any damage which requires immediate repairs, e.g. a leaking roof, call your insurers and get their agreement before making repairs, if possible, or you may damage the evidence. Or take photos if you can't contact the insurers. Bear in mind that if the insurers agree to making repairs, it does not automatically mean they agree to pay the claim.
- Where the building has been damaged, get builders to estimate the cost of repairs, and ask what they think was the cause of the damage. Preferably get this in writing. If you disagree with the builder's verdict, get another builder's opinion.
- Inform the police of a burglary immediately.
- Call your insurance company and ask them to send you a claim form.
- Check very carefully to discover what is missing. Often people only notice that something is missing weeks after a burglary. When making a claim make clear that the list of items stolen is 'so far as we can see at present'.
- Check your insurance policy to make sure that

items damaged and the cause of damage are covered by your policy.

- Look out any receipts or valuations for stolen items.
- Find out the cost of replacing any lost items. Try to find the cheapest equivalent but do not accept anything of a lower quality than you had before.
- Do not exaggerate the claim. One of the main reasons why reduced offers are made is that the insurers think the claim was exaggerated. They may even refuse the claim altogether.

If your claim is refused or reduced

- If your claim isn't accepted in full, complain to the head of the company first. Be cautious about accepting offers of less than the amount you are claiming. You may be asked to complete a form agreeing to 'full and final' settlement. Don't do this if you wish to claim more.
- If the dispute is over the cause of the damage, get together evidence to support your case. For example, if there is a dispute over what caused something to break, find out how old the item was and its normal natural life. If necessary, get expert witnesses, e.g. electricians, builders and so on, to look at the damage and give an opinion.
- If the dispute is over the value of damaged items, and you don't have any valuations, get new estimated valuations by describing the items to experts – e.g. proprietors of antique shops, electrical goods shops etc.
- If you are accused of making a fraudulent claim, for example, if you claim for stolen or destroyed items and the insurers dispute that the items claimed for ever existed, get witness statements from people who have seen them, or try to find photographs showing them.
- If the disputed loss is very large, you can hire a loss assessor to try to collect as much evidence on your side as possible. Loss assessors usually work for a percentage of the final insurance pay out. Contact the Institute of Public Loss Assessors (see **Addresses**).

- If the insurance company sends a loss adjuster to examine the damage, ask for a copy of his or her report. Insurance companies are not required to show you this, but some will do so.
- If you are still not happy with the way you have been treated, you can go to court or to one of the complaints schemes (see page 197).

Your insurance company can refuse to pay your claim if they think that you failed to take 'due care', i.e. reasonable precautions to prevent loss or damage, e.g., if you leave a window open and are burgled.

CAR INSURANCE

Third party   This is the minimum legal requirement for cars. It covers you for injuries to other people (including passengers in your own car) and their property, but does not cover you for any damage to you or your vehicle.

Third party,   In addition to the above, this gives cover if your car
fire and theft   catches fire or is stolen.

Comprehensive   This is the most expensive form of insurance but, in addition to the above, it covers you for accidental damage to your own car (even if it was your fault) and personal accident benefit if the policy-holder dies or is permanently disabled.

What's   Car radios and hi-fis are usually covered up to a
covered   limited amount, around £300. Car telephones are often not covered at all. Cover for items stolen from the car is usually limited to around £150. If you are

going to carry expensive items around with you, you should insure them specially on your house contents policy. However, if you leave valuable items behind in a car and they are stolen, an insurer may consider that you have not taken due care and may refuse to pay your claim.

A few policies also cover you for the cost of a hire car while yours is being repaired or replaced. Some will also pay for overnight accommodation if you are unable to complete your journey after an accident.

Many car insurance policies also provide legal expenses cover. If not, you can buy it on its own from most car insurance brokers. If you are injured in an accident or suffer any other loss which isn't covered by your insurance and the accident was caused by another person, you can sue that person for compensation. Legal expenses insurance will pay for the cost of doing this.

Money-saving tips

- You can reduce car insurance premiums by limiting the number of people who are covered under the policy (even cheaper if they are all over 25) and by paying a voluntary excess, say the first £100 of any claim.
- If you don't claim on your car insurance you will gradually build up a no-claims discount. This will usually be a 20 per cent discount after one year of claim-free driving, 40 per cent after two years, 50 per cent after three years and 60 per cent after four.
- If your insurance company has to pay a claim for you, regardless of whether or not you were to blame, you will lose all or part of your no-claims discount. (But, if you make a claim after an accident for which someone else was to blame, *so long as you can identify the person who caused the accident and can prove it was his or her fault*, your insurance company will be able to claim back the cost of any repairs to your car from the insurers of the person who caused the accident. This means you don't lose your no-claims discount.)

- You can pay an extra premium to protect your no-claims discount. This means you won't lose your no-claims discount *unless* you make more than the specified number of claims in a certain time period (e.g. no more than three claims in five years).

WHAT YOUR INSURERS WON'T PAY FOR

- Expenses incurred in making your claim, e.g. cost of stamps and phone calls.

- Cost of alternative transport (unless your policy is one of the few which does cover this).

- Personal injury (if your injuries are caused by another driver, then he or she is liable to pay your compensation).

- Loss of earnings.

- Compensation for inconvenience.

HOLIDAY INSURANCE

You will need to be covered against cancellation or having to cut short your holiday, for personal accident, for personal liability for injury or damage caused to other people and their property, and for medical expenses where necessary (not within the European Community whose countries have a reciprocal agreement to provide medical treatment).

If you are likely to be taking part in a dangerous sport, such as rock climbing or deep-sea diving, you should have specific insurance against injury. You should also have your luggage and personal possessions insured.

Check carefully any policy for exclusion clauses which might conceivably affect your holiday. Also check to make sure the insurance company is a member of a complaints scheme (see **Addresses**) – preferably the Insurance Ombudsman Bureau (see also **Holidays** section).

COMPLAINTS SCHEMES

There are two main complaints schemes for insurance disputes – the Insurance Ombudsman Bureau and the Personal Insurance Arbitration Service (PIAS). Both are free and most companies belong to one or the other (it will say which in your policy document).

If you complain to PIAS you must agree to abide by the decision and surrender any right to take the dispute to court if you are unhappy with its decision. With the Insurance Ombudsman Bureau, the decision is binding on the company up to £100,000, but if you are not happy you can reject the decision and go to court.

Neither will take your case if:

- it concerns a complaint against someone else's insurance company
- it concerns a policy relating to business
- you have started legal proceedings
- you are complaining because a company has refused to insure you, or has set exceptionally high premiums.

The procedure for complaining to the Insurance Ombudsman is set out below.

Insurance Ombudsman

- Complain first, in writing, to the manager of your insurance company.
- Write to the Ombudsman within six weeks of getting a final reply from the company if not satisfied.
- The Ombudsman may require further information. He or she may try to settle by giving advice; if that does not work, a formal decision will be made.

Personal
Insurance
Arbitration
Service (PIAS)

The complaints procedure in this case is set out below.

- Try the company's complaints system first.
- If this produces no results, you can apply to PIAS for arbitration (the insurance company must also agree).
- An arbiter will then examine the case from both sides; all three parties can ask for an informal hearing.

(See **Addresses**.)

Holidays

- Medical matters
- Guardian angel
- Be secure
- When things go wrong
- Passport panic
- Before you go
- Luggage lore

The problems created by going on holiday can make you wonder whether it's worth all the hassle. But failure to take some simple precautions could mean you come home to chaos. Write yourself a checklist of things that need doing before you go.

MEDICAL MATTERS

Check that anyone on regular medication has sufficient supplies of it to last through the holiday, and ask your GP or pharmacist what you should do in a particular country if you should lose it. Carry vital medical supplies in your hand luggage.

Check the standard insurance issued by your tour operator (it usually excludes any pre-existing illness). Take out your own insurance in addition if you have a pre-existing illness (see also **Insurance** section).

Apply for form E111 well in advance of your trip. You can get a copy from any main post office. It entitles you to medical treatment in EC countries. If you have a pre-existing illness you can receive free or reduced-cost treatment in other EC countries by applying on form E112. Get your GP to confirm your condition and send the statement with an E111 to the Department of Health (see **Addresses**).

Form SA35, from the Department of Health, lists all the immunisations you need for visiting different countries.

PASSPORT PANIC

Getting a new passport can take time, particularly in busy holiday months. Ideally, make a diary note about three months before it runs out.

If you urgently need to travel abroad and your passport is about to or has expired, there are two options:

British Visitors Passport You can get a British Visitors Passport form from a post office; fill it in and obtain an on-the-spot passport which enables you to travel to European Community countries and Scandinavia. You require proof of identity, proof of nationality, plus passport photographs.

Or you can visit one of the six passport offices in the UK (in Belfast, Glasgow, Liverpool, London, Newport and Peterborough) and plead your special case which will usually be considered sympathetically if, for example, there has been a death overseas or an urgent business problem. You need to fill in the form and have passport photographs which have been countersigned as instructed on the form. With this method you could have a passport within the day.

GUARDIAN ANGEL

Ideally, you want your home to look as if you, or at any rate someone, is living in it. Installing a home-sitter is one answer but you need to be sure that he or she is going to prove reliable and do things such as switch on the burglar alarm and feed the tropical fish. You can use someone supplied by a home-sitting agency (which should have taken up references) but the total cost will be quite high. However, it does give you the peace of mind that someone is living in your home and if you would otherwise incur the cost of kennelling pets and perhaps paying someone to water your garden you might think it worthwhile. Alternatively, you might have a friend (or a friend of a friend) who, in return for free accommodation and perhaps food, would be prepared to undertake your requirements. If you do opt for a live-in home-sitter from an agency, ask to interview him or her first. Reliable agencies are happy to arrange this. Some home-sitters operate as couples; check also whether you have to pay for food for two. Check too that your house contents insurance policy covers potential damage or that the agency has a policy dealing with this. (For a list of agencies see **Addresses**). You could also ask a trusted neighbour to pop in on a regular basis and perform small tasks, such as picking mail off the doormat and watering the houseplants.

Whoever you entrust with looking after your home should be given detailed information about how to contact you if there is a crisis, who your insurers are (in case of a burglary) and how to operate any security system you have.

BEFORE YOU GO

Watering houseplants

To reduce the need for too much watering, or if you can't find anyone to do it, move houseplants somewhere cool, water them well, then cover them with large polythene bags, secured round the pots, to create a mini greenhouse that keeps water in the atmosphere. Don't do this with furry-leaved plants which may rot.

For long absences invest in capillary matting (from garden centres and some florists). Stand the plants on the matting and put one end of it in a large bowl or bucket of water. The water will 'wick' up the matting and keep the soil moist. Don't put the matting in a sink or basin of water unless the plug is a perfect fit or the water will gradually drain away.

Pet plans

Cold-water and tropical fish can be left with vacation food for three or four weeks with no ill-effects. Small caged creatures, such as hamsters and guinea-pigs, can usually stay with your friends. Dogs and cats will need boarding kennels if you are away for more than a few days. Being fed and walked by a neighbour for a long period means they won't starve, but they will get lonely, and cats may stray and possibly adopt a new family.

Pay up in advance Anticipate any bills that are likely to be due in your absence and pay them in advance. Postdate the cheque if you're on a tight budget, but remember to post it. You don't want to get home and find your phone cut off or a whacking interest charge on your credit-card account.

Switching off If you are leaving your home empty, make it as difficult as possible for things to go wrong. Turn off the water supply to the washing-machine and dishwasher. In winter, turn off the stopcock for the main water supply but leave the central heating on low. In summer, turn off the water heater. Turn off the gas and as much electrical equipment as possible. Remove plugs from sockets. Don't turn off the freezer. Disconnect the TV and video unless you are specifically recording a programme during your absence. Check that you have backed up everything on your computer.

BE SECURE

Check that all your security devices are working properly, particularly those which operate on timers. Check the exterior of your home to ensure that no ladders or implements which could be used to break in and gain access to windows are lying around. Cancel newspapers and milk deliveries: you don't want to tell would-be intruders that your home is unoccupied. Inside the home put away small valuable items such as jewellery and ornaments and make sure any spare house keys are concealed.

Cut the grass just before you leave and lock the shed and garage.

Leave keys (without your name and address on the ring) with a trusted neighbour. A free leaflet from the Home Office, *Peace of mind while you're away*, is available from police stations or by phoning 071-273-2193. See also **Well secured** section.

LUGGAGE LORE

- Don't put your home address on the labels of your suitcases. Use that of your office or a relation who you know is not away. Information revealing that you are away can be used by thieves who spot your labels.
- Don't overfill your luggage or it may burst open. Use a strap on suitcases.
- Make sure your luggage is insured for its correct value. If you are travelling with expensive items, for example, photographic equipment, you will need special cover.
- If your luggage is lost in transit you must report it immediately. If you are travelling on a package holiday, your tour operator should be able to help with this.
- At an airport, fill in a Property Irregularity Form (PIR), which your insurers will require you to do and which also helps the airline staff trace your bags.
- Luggage lost on a train has usually been stolen and you should report the fact to the rail authorities on arrival.

If you are stranded without essential items, you can purchase what you need after 12 hours and claim the cost on insurance. Don't go wild: claims for complete replacement are unlikely to be met; simply replace the bare necessities.

WHEN THINGS GO WRONG

If something goes wrong with your holiday you should complain and insist on compensation. You might need to claim for the following.
- Incorrect description in the brochure. This might include a swimming-pool described but not yet built or a statement such as 'within walking distance of the sea' when it is two miles away.
- Excessive noise. This could be claimed if your hotel or apartment is next to a building site or a very noisy nightclub.
- Overcharging. When you book you should be told the total charge for your rooms, whether this includes bath, shower, toilet, etc.

- Overbooking. If a company has overbooked and requires you to go to another hotel or apartment you have a case if the replacement is not up to the standard you have booked.
- If you have to make a complaint, follow this procedure.
Report the problem to the hotel/apartment block manager or to the tour operator's representative and see if your problem can be sorted out on the spot. If this does not work, see if other holidaymakers are similarly affected and get together, exchanging home addresses. Make notes and, where appropriate, take photographs which could provide useful evidence. On your return, within 28 days, send a written complaint (keeping a copy) to the firm you booked with. If you still get no joy, either pursue the case in the county court (the small claims procedure may be used for claims of up to £1000), or if the offending firm is a member, take up the matter with the Association of British Travel Agents (ABTA) – see **Addresses.**

Addresses

Association of British Insurers
51–55 Gresham Street
London EC2V 7HQ
Tel 071-600 3333

Association of British Travel Agents (ABTA)
55–57 Newman Street
London W1P 4AH
Tel 071–637 2444

British Association of Removers
3 Churchill Court
58 Station Road
North Harrow
Middlesex HA2 7SA
Tel 081–861 3331

British Board of Agrément (BBA)
PO Box 195
Bucknall Lane
Garston
Watford
Hertfordshire WD2 7NG
Tel (0923) 670844

British Decorators Association
6 Haywra Street
Harrogate
North Yorkshire HG1 5BL
Tel (0423) 567292

British Insurance and Investment Brokers Association
BIIBA House
14 Bevis Marks
London EC3A 7NT
Tel 071–623 9043

British Pest Control Association
3 St James Court
Friar Gate
Derby
Derbyshire DE1 1ZU
Tel (0332) 294288

The British Red Cross Society
9 Grosvenor Crescent
London SW1X 7EJ
Tel 071–235 5454

British Security Industry Association (BSIA)
Security House
Barbourne Road
Worcester
Hereford & Worcester WR1 1RS
Tel (0905) 21464

British Standards Institution
Information Department
Linford Wood
Milton Keynes
Buckinghamshire MK14 6LE
Tel (0908) 226888

Building Employers Confederation
82 New Cavendish Street
London W1M 8AD
Tel 071–580 5588

Council for Registered Gas Installers (CORGI)
4 Elmwood
Chineham Business Park
Crockford Lane
Basingstoke
Hampshire RG24 0WG
Tel (0256) 707060

Cyclists' Touring Club
Cotterell House
69 Meadrow
Godalming
Surrey GU7 3HS
Tel (0483) 417217

Driver Vehicle Licensing Centre
Swansea
SA99 1BN

Department of Health
International Relations Unit
(for form E112)
Room 313
Hannibal House
Elephant and Castle
London SE1 6TE
Tel 071–972 1919

Electrical Contractors Association (ECA)
ESCA House
34 Palace Court
Bayswater
London W2 4JG
Tel 071–229 1266

Electrical Contractors Association of Scotland
Bush House
Bush Estate
Midlothian
Lothian EH26 0SB
Tel 031–445 5577

Energy Action Grants Agency
PO Box 1NG
Newcastle upon Tyne
NE99 1NG
Freephone (0800) 181667

External Wall Insulation Association
PO Box 12
Haslemere
Surrey GU27 3AH
Tel (0428) 654011

Glass and Glazing Federation
44–48 Borough High Street
London SE1 1XB
Tel 071–403 7177

Guild of Master Craftsmen
166 High Street
Lewes
East Sussex BN7 1XU
Tel (0273) 478449

Heating and Ventilating Contractors Association (HVCA)
34 Palace Court
Bayswater
London W2 4JG
Tel 071–229 2488

Home-sitting agencies
(operating countrywide)

Home and Pet Care Ltd
Tel (06998) 515

Homesitters Ltd
Tel (0442) 891188

Housewatch Ltd
Tel (0279) 78412

Stanley's Caring Service
Tel (0424) 420762

Universal Aunts Ltd
Tel 071–351 5767

Institute of Plumbing
64 Station Lane
Hornchurch
Essex RM12 6NB
Tel (0708) 472791

Institute of Public Loss Assessors
14 Red Lion Street
Chesham
Buckinghamshire HP5 1HB
Tel (0494) 782342

The Insurance Ombudsman
City Gate One
135 Park Street
London SE1 9EA
Tel 071–928 7600

Mailing Preference Service
Freepost 22
London W1E 7EZ
Tel 071–738 1625

National Approval Council for Security Systems (NACOSS)
Queensgate House
14 Cookham Road
Maidenhead
Berkshire SL6 8AJ
Tel (0628) 37512

National Association of Plumbing, Heating and Mechanical Services
   Contractors (NAPHMSC)
14 & 15 Ensign House
Ensign Business Centre
Westwood Way
Coventry
Warwickshire CV4 8JA
Tel (0203) 470626

National Cavity Insulation Association
PO Box 12
Haslemere
Surrey GU27 3AH
Tel (0428) 654011

National Federation of Roofing Contractors
24 Weymouth Street
London W1N 3FA
Tel 071–436 0387

National Inspection Council for Electrical Installation Contracting (NICEIC)
Vintage House
37 Albert Embankment
London SE1 7UJ
Tel 071–735 1322

PIAS
Personal Insurance Arbitration Service
24 Angel Gate
City Road
London EC1V 2RS
Tel 071–837 4483

Royal Institute of British Architects
66 Portland Place
London W1N 4AD
Tel 071–580 5533

Royal Institute of Chartered Surveyors
12 Great George Street
Parliament Square
London SW1P 3AD
Tel 071–222 7000

St John Ambulance
1 Grosvenor Crescent
London SW1X 7EF
Tel 071–235 5231

Scottish and Northern Ireland Plumbing Employers Federation
2 Walker Street
Edinburgh
Lothian EH3 7LB
Tel 031–225 2255

Vitreous Enamel Development Council
Charnwood
Frenze Road
Diss
Norfolk IP22 3PB
Tel (0379) 650340

Weights and measures

METRIC AND IMPERIAL MEASUREMENTS

Length

Centimetres		Inches
2.540	1	0.394
5.080	2	0.787
7.620	3	1.181
10.160	4	1.575
12.700	5	1.969
15.240	6	2.362
17.780	7	2.756
20.320	8	3.150
22.860	9	3.543

Metres		Yards
0.914	1	1.094
1.829	2	2.187
2.743	3	3.281
3.658	4	4.374
4.572	5	5.468
5.486	6	6.562
6.401	7	7.655
7.315	8	8.749
8.230	9	9.843

Kilometres		Miles
1.609	1	0.621
3.219	2	1.243
4.828	3	1.864
6.437	4	2.485
8.047	5	3.107
9.656	6	3.728
11.265	7	4.350
12.875	8	4.971
14.484	9	5.592

Volume

Litres		Gallons
4.546	1	0.220
9.092	2	0.440
13.638	3	0.660
18.184	4	0.880
22.730	5	1.100
27.276	6	1.320
31.822	7	1.540
36.368	8	1.760
40.914	9	1.980

Weight

Kilograms		Pounds
0.454	1	2.205
0.907	2	4.409
1.361	3	6.614
1.814	4	8.819
2.268	5	11.023
2.722	6	13.228
3.175	7	15.432
3.629	8	17.637
4.082	9	19.842

Area

Sq metres		Sq yards
0.836	1	1.196
1.672	2	2.392
2.508	3	3.588
3.345	4	4.784
4.181	5	5.980
5.017	6	7.176
5.853	7	8.372
6.689	8	9.568
7.525	9	10.764

Easy conversions

Metres into yards
add one-tenth

Yards into metres
deduct one-tenth

Kilometres into miles
multiply by 5 and divide by 8

Miles into kilometres
multiply by 8 and divide by 5

Litres into pints
multiply by 7 and divide by 4

Pints into litres
multiply by 4 and divide by 7

Litres into gallons
multiply by 2 and divide by 9

Gallons into litres
multiply by 9 and divide by 2

Kilograms into pounds
divide by 9 and multiply by 20

Pounds into kilograms
divide by 20 and multiply by 9

Fahrenheit to centigrade
deduct 32, multiply by 5, divide by 9

Centigrade to Fahrenheit
multiply by 9, divide by 5, add 32.

IMPERIAL/METRIC EQUIVALENTS

Weight (solid)

1 oz	=	28 grams
1 pound	=	454 grams
1 stone	=	6.3 kilograms
1 cwt	=	50.8 kilograms
100 grams	=	3½ oz
200 grams	=	7 oz
1 kilogram	=	2 lbs 3 oz
1 tonne	=	0.9842 ton

Length

1 inch	=	2.5 centimetres
1 foot	=	30 centimetres
1 yard	=	91 centimetres
1 mile	=	1,609 metres
1 centimetre	=	0.4 inches
1 metre	=	3 yards 3 inches
1 kilometre	=	1,093 yards
1 kilometre	=	0.6214 mile

Fluid measures conversion

Metric	Imperial	US
5 millilitres	1 teaspoon	1 teaspoon
15 millilitres	1 tablespoon	1 tablespoon
120 millilitres	4 fl oz	½ cup
150 millilitres	¼ pint (5 fl oz)	⅔ cup
225 millilitres	8 fl oz	1 cup
300 millilitres	½ pint (10 fl oz)	1¼ cups
450 millilitres	¾ pint (15 fl oz)	2 cups
600 millilitres	1 pint (20 fl oz)	2½ cups
750 millilitres	24 fl oz	3 cups

(*See also* page 19)

Index

'*ff*' denotes numerous subsequent references